# THE MODERN LEADER

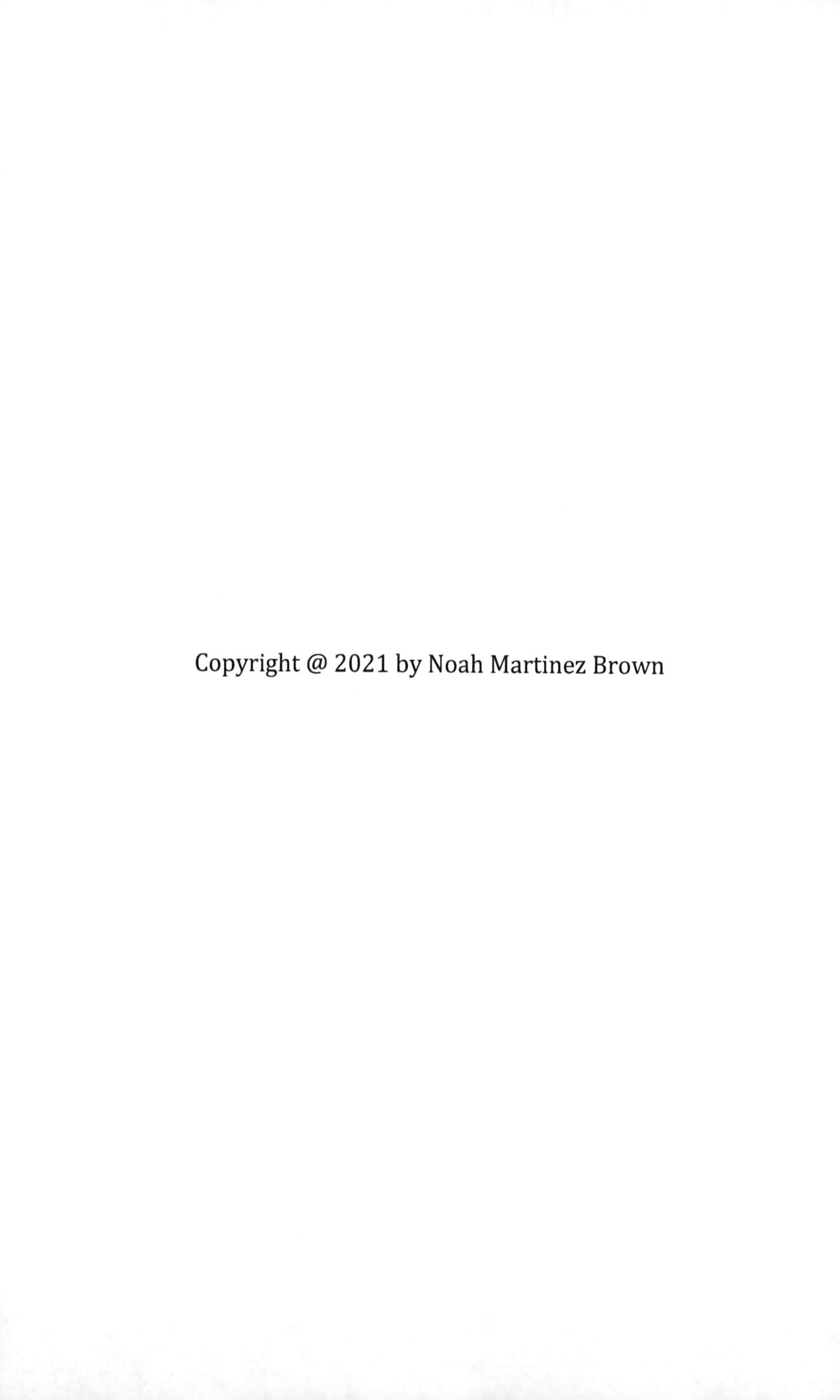

# Contents

# INTRODUCTION

Hello dear esteemed reader, it is with utmost gratitude and pleasure that I thank you for picking up this book.

You've taken a big step towards self-improvement and I thank you for that, I also thank you for deciding to be a better leader-not just for others but for yourself as well. To lead is to serve, and in order to lead others, you need to first be a able to lead yourself. So, thank you once again. I hope you enjoy this book and I hope it's detailed enough to satisfy your thirst for improvement. LET'S GET STARTED.

Leadership is a skill set; it is not some inborn natural talent like many people say. It is a skill that can be studied, practised, taught, and in adverse cases, "unlearnt". "True leadership is a very scarce character; it's rare to find great leaders nowadays. It's not developed solely from weekend workshops or manuals."

That leads to the question, What do influential leaders do?" Leaders create strategies, encourage employees, define a mission, and create communities. If you ask a group of people that are savvy in business this simple question, "What is the duty of a leaders?" If the group is experienced, you'll probably receive one response: the leader's sole responsibility is to achieve results.

But how do leaders do it? It's an age-old question about what leaders can and should do to inspire the most satisfactory performance from their employees and other executives. In recent years, this fascinating question has birthed an entirely new industry: many so-called "leadership experts" have made a living out of assessing and mentoring executives, all in the hopes of developing other corporate executives who can achieve ambitious goals, whether they are strategic, financial, organisational, or all three.

Despite this, many people and organisations struggle to lead their employees effectively. One explanation is that, until recently, certain quantitative studies have shown which specific leadership behaviours produce positive outcomes. Experts in leadership provide guidance based on inference, history, and intuition. Sometimes such counsel is spot on, and other times it is valid. However, new studies based on a random sample of over 3000 executives drawn from a database of more than 20,000 executives globally removes much of the mystique around effective leadership. Six distinct leadership styles emerged from the study, each stemming from different aspects of emotional intelligence. Individually, the styles appear to have a direct and distinct influence on their respective companies, position, divisions, or team's working environment, hence its financial success. Perhaps most importantly, the research shows that the most effective leaders do not rely on just one leadership style; they employ a variety of styles throughout the week—seamlessly and in varying degrees—depending on the business circumstances. Consider the styles like a collection of clubs in a golf pro's bag.

During the course of a game, the pro selects clubs based on the shot's requirements. He has to think about his choice occasionally, although it is generally intuitive. The pro recognises the task at hand, quickly pulls out the appropriate tool, and puts it to work in a beautiful manner. That's also how high-impact leaders work.

What are the six leadership styles? None of these will come as a surprise to anyone who has worked in the office before. Indeed, anybody who leads, serves, or, as is the case with most of us, does both will certainly resonate with each style based only on its name and brief description. Leaders that use coercion want quick obedience and many of their employees would probably despise them. Authoritative leaders inspire others to work toward a common goal but sometimes push it too hard and end up forcing works on their employees. Leaders who are connected establish emotional ties and peace. Democratic leaders achieve agreement through involving their followers. Leaders who set the pace demand excellence and personality from their employees. Leaders who are coaches build individuals for the future.

Close your eyes and envision a coworker who employs one of these approaches. At least one of these is likely to be used by you or someone around you. So, what's unique about this study is its implications for action. For starters, it provides a detailed understanding of how various leadership styles influence performance and outcomes. Second, it specifies when a manager should move from one method to the other. It also strongly implies that switching can be done in a variety of ways. The research also discovered that different components of emotional intelligence are responsible for different leadership styles.

When you take up a book like this, it's probable that your motivations are at least partially selfish. I don't mean "selfish" in a negative context. I'm assuming you want to improve yourself so you can be a better leader and accomplish something individually. This strikes me as a great goal. Personal development is beneficial in almost any situation. Your life improves as you improve yourself. But it's also more than that: Your personal growth is inextricably linked to the advancement of any group or initiative in which you participate, whether it's a family, a team, a corporation, or—if you want to go big—the human species. We all belong within a huge configuration of bigger wholes, as we explored in our examination of the responsibility attitude. As a result, as we grow, so does everything we come into contact with.

This is the Trojan Horse of Intelligent Leadership in my opinion. You may be initially motivated by the prospect of developing your leadership skills in order to advance in your career or achieve more personal achievement. But, at the end of the day, genuinely exceptional leaders recognise that this evolution is not about them. They learn — and eventually internalise — that the most significant impact their leadership growth can have is on the cultures in which they find themselves. Leaders, whether they like it or not, are guardians of culture.

So, what exactly is culture? That's a challenging topic to answer because culture is inherently enigmatic and difficult to describe. So, to illustrate, I'll use an anatomical metaphor.

I occasionally work out with a personal trainer, and she constantly stresses the necessity of warming up properly before each workout. She emphasises the significance of freeing up my "myofascial tissue" in particular. Myofascial tissue is a thin, virtually invisible layer of fibrous tissue that surrounds all of our muscles and bones, for those of you who aren't up on the newest exercise warm-up trends. It's incredibly powerful despite its thinness. It preserves our muscles and bones by actually holding our body together. Consider it like a net: if there are knots or bunches of net that aren't moving freely, the bones and muscles beneath the net are physically trapped, or tied up, and are unable to operate effectively. So, as my trainer likes to say, if you want to unleash more movement in your body, you must first loosen up the myofascial tissue. This is generally performed by slowly massaging important areas in our musculoskeletal system with a firm foam roller, which is a painful process. It may be painful, but it works. And I'm now convinced of the critical function that myofascial tissue plays in total bodily wellness.

I consider "culture" to be the myofascial tissue of every organisational structure, whether small (like a family or a team) or large (like a global corporation or even a nation). The culture of any organisation is typically unseen to its members, owing to the fact that it is complex. It's the sum total of everyone's shared values and ideas, relational structures, and norms (both conscious and unconscious) about what's right and wrong, good and terrible, acceptable and unacceptable. Culture, like myofascial tissue, binds your company together and determines almost every aspect of it.

Culture is an intangible quality that pervades the environment of your home, office, or community. And, strangely enough, it's harder to detect when things are going well. When your culture is humming, it brings out the best in everyone else in your company or group. The degree of lightness or creativity permeating everything and everyone in your group is a hint to measuring the quality of your organization's culture. Members report higher levels of satisfaction, and the bottom-line outcomes you may produce as a group increase.

It's equally possible that the reverse is true. It might seem like a heaviness or tension in the air of your company when anything is wrong with your culture, as when your myofascial tissue is hard or all knotted up and needs a good rolling. Morale is poor, infighting and power conflicts are prevalent, and individuals are more concerned with what they can receive from the firm rather than what they can contribute, all of which leads to lower productivity—and profitability.

The culture of New York City after the September 11 attacks is one example that comes to mind that serves to make the notion of culture apparent. Many people said that the horrors of that day produced a real feeling of shared purpose that pulled people together. The typical boundaries that individuals build around themselves were dismantled. Strangers felt as if they were brothers and sisters to me. Those events altered the culture of a whole city, at least momentarily, and pushed people into action. The abrupt difference in their own cultural experience exposed something to New Yorkers that they probably hadn't given much consideration to previously. Now, it's critical to understand that it doesn't require a dramatic occurrence or a catastrophe to bring culture into focus or to foster a healthy culture in a family, business, or nation. This is just an example to get you thinking about how you "see" culture in your own life.

"A "Bossy/Stalin-like" attitude to commanding workers and peers will not produce positive outcomes in the workplace or in life. Rather, real and effective leaders today rely on the Essentials of Effective Leadership, which will be addressed in this book, whether they lead from the C-suite (a phrase frequently used to refer to a company's top executives), the assembly line, the PTO, or in personal relationships.

True leaders understand how to make ethical decisions in the face of real-life situations. They understand what it takes to gain loyalty and respect, motivate via compassion, build strong connections, improve open communication, and help others develop leadership abilities. They also realize that they are not the centre of the universe. As a result, they find personal fulfilment in whatever they accomplish. Whatever the conditions or economic situation, those who know and appreciate the basic tenets of personal and professional leadership constantly come out on top, increasing productivity, profitability, and achieving the organization's end result.

Aside from layoffs, job satisfaction is at its lowest point in two decades. CEOs are concerned about "developing future leaders." Middle managers worry about a lack of top-down leadership. The economic downturn appears to have harmed motivation and direction. All of these circumstances, however, point to a far bigger issue: a general absence of true leadership in an organization and even beyond.

This book hopes to help instil true leadership spirit, it is written to be an easy-to-understand guide on developing leaders in the business and in life. Almost everyone may benefit from this book's understanding of what it takes to inspire and lead. This book will exemplify how real leaders serve their employees, with the right direction and guidance, how they build and empower teams, then quietly stand back and observe as others achieve success, which in turn creates the leader's own success, with the help of real-life stories and advice from a diverse range of pace-setters.

Put the academic definitions aside and replace them with a list of leadership "styles," such as transactional, trans-motivational, or charismatic. Real Leaders Don't Boss and this book will educate readers who aspire to be great leaders not to boss, it will teach how to inspire others, instruct and mentor them, and assist them in meeting their professional and personal objectives while also helping the company achieve its goals.

For many years of my life, I have been a student of true knowledge, an inquisitive fellow seeking out ways to improve myself anf others around me and I've realized that true leadership is an essential trait that everyone should try to build. I've studied the ideas and principles of real leaders in a variety of sectors and enterprises, as well as in government. I've worked as a C-suite executive, a communications expert, university professor, hospital executive, administrator, consultant, writer, columnist, and entrepreneur. Along the way, I've met or worked with a lot of world-class leaders both in the public and private sectors. My leadership style has evolved into a one-of-a-kind blend of personal insight, vision, historical perspective, varied professional experience, and military discipline."

Many managers make the error of thinking that leadership style is a personality trait rather than a strategic decision. Rather than picking the style that best matches their temperament, people should consider which style best meets the needs of a specific circumstance and the needs of their employees.

Self-awareness, self-regulation, drive, empathy, and social competence are among the emotional intelligence characteristics that the most effective leaders possess, according to research. There are six primary leadership styles, each of which employs the fundamental components of emotional intelligence in various combinations. The finest leaders aren't experts in just one style of leadership; they're adept at several and can flip between them depending on the situation.

This book is about a naturally occurring pattern, a style of thinking, acting, and communicating that allows certain leaders to inspire others. Although these "natural-born leaders" may have been born with the ability to inspire, they are not the only ones who possess it. This pattern is one that we can all learn. Any leader or organisation may inspire people, both inside and outside their company, to assist in promoting their ideas and goals. With a little discipline and conscious effort, we can all improve our leadership skills.

# CHAPTER 1:
# LEADERSHIP DEFINED

A leader is anyone in a decision-making capacity, formal or informal, who advances the strategic goals of the organisation, who contributes mightily to institutional performance, and who treats people fairly, honestly, and compassionately. Real leadership goes well beyond that textbook definition, however. Real leaders create the right conditions for others to lead. Here are some of the characteristic traits of what a good leader should be:

True leaders don't boss. They want to do the right thing and contribute to something greater than themselves.

True leaders speak with clarity, honesty, and directness, and they listen well.

True leaders are one-of-a-kind individuals. Their enthusiasm is reflected in the firm's culture.

True leaders do not lord it over their subordinates. They have a calm demeanour, yet they have zero tolerance for bullies who disrupt performance and morale in any way.

True leaders value and assist everyone they lead, both in and out of the office or anywhere, even at home.

True leaders understand when to step aside and when to let others shine.

True leaders are warm and receptive. They're approachable and humble.

True leaders understand the distinction between character and integrity, as well as why both are necessary for success.

There are many "leaders" today who manifest some of these traits; a few demonstrate all of them. The great differentiator, though, is that real leaders embrace *all* of these principles *all* of the time. That's a truism whether it involves leaders in business, government, the military, or private life. In the following pages, I'll talk in-depth about each of these attributes, what they mean, and how you, too, can learn to embrace them. Almost all of us have the potential to lead in some capacity; we simply need to learn how to allow that potential to surface.

True leaders are hard to come by in today's fast-paced, money-driven society. So many fake gurus and imposters have taken their place, seeking rapid gratification in the shape of speedy (and unsustainable) bottom-line success.

These wannabe-leaders flaunt rigid controls and "bossiness" instead of passionate leadership. They seek to drive employees through dominance rather than devotion, and opt for personal glory over the success and interests of others. In part, today's struggling corporate performance, as well as the trend toward dissatisfaction in the workplace, reflect these shortcomings in leadership.

Today's realities, especially with the rocky economic environment and the growing numbers of Millennials (also known as Generation Y, those workers born somewhere between 1980 and 2000) joining the workforce, calls for leadership done right. It demands real leaders who can, and do, make profound differences in the lives of those with whom they interact, who help others achieve greatness in the workplace and in life, and who boost professional and personal bottom lines in the process.

Even strong companies must learn to become more adept at handling marketplace turbulence faster and more skilfully, or their leaders will risk losing their edge, and the company its strength, over the competition. Real leaders recognise that they must maintain the success that has already been accomplished, and the culture, integrity, and brand that defines it. Only then can they continue to institute change successfully and propel a company forward.

The leadership gap today is painfully evident. Workers are not happy with their jobs. Middle managers berate the lack of top-level leadership—one that provides motivation, fosters dedication, promotes recognition, and offers long-term direction. Even corporate leaders recognise the disconnect and its threat to future economic recovery and growth. After all, leaders are needed not only to weather an economic storm, but afterward, to grow and improve battered companies for the future.

Great leaders can be born into a family of leaders—the Kennedys, for example—but being born into a family of leaders is no guarantee of success. True leaders are cultivated over time, as they learn from their mistakes and are nourished and developed.

Too often we hear things such as "he (or she) is a natural-born leader." A person may, indeed, have the make-up, temperament, patience, and vision to lead, but without the right attitude, experience, approach, and training, that individual's "knack" for leadership doesn't translate into real leadership.

Whether leaders are born or made is "an age old question that has dogged academicians and practitioners alike for centuries.

The answer is they are born and also made. But leadership can be learnt and achieved by all. We have all heard the stories of natural leaders who, after an undistinguished career, emerge a hero in combat environments by leading their men out of danger or to take an objective. They instill confidence and courage in others who then find the strength to continue to fight and help others. Winston Churchill, I believe, fell into this category. He was pilloried at times for his perceived lack of leadership but as prime minister rallied the people and saved England during World War II. He was then promptly thrown out of office. But, I believe that more leaders are made than born. There are leadership academies everywhere. Most prep schools advertise that they develop future leaders. Our colleges and universities pick up this mantra and it dominates their marketing material. And, of course, the military promises, in its multimillion-dollar recruitment efforts, to build tomorrow's leaders.

The majority of true leaders aren't born with an intrinsic aptitude that turns them into magnets that draw people to them. They may be under pressure to rise beyond their current status or environment, or they may have an inborn desire to help others and do something special. However, most leaders grow and polish their leadership talents on the battlefield of life, where they discover their drive, passion, and knowledge. Through trial and error, winning and losing, a leader's self-confidence grows, aplomb develops, and risk-taking becomes a more accepted path. Observation of other leaders in action and service to others often becomes very important.

Honing those leadership skills can happen outside the workplace, too. One of the many leadership "platforms" helpful to me was my college fraternity. Serving my fraternity brothers in different roles afforded numerous types of leadership training. I learned quickly how to deal with adversity and constructive criticism, as well as how to improve, grow, and handle increased responsibility. Perhaps most important, the significance of serving others was reinforced time and again, as was the value of a close-knit and open-minded community.

Being chosen by my peers to be captain of a varsity sports team was also an important learning experience for me. As captains are normally chosen to help inspire and energise a team, I saw this opportunity as a test of my leadership skills. I realised I had to not only step up my performance as an athlete but also to set an example by the way I practiced, helped younger players, and reinforced the coaches' goals for the season. My coaches instilled in me the belief that effective captains helped develop and teach the less experienced among us just as business leaders strengthen their employees' skills. Whether you are a captain of a sports team, an academic decathlon, a debate team, or a work team, you learn to be a better leader by practical experience.

What comes to mind when you hear the word "leader"? You may draw up an image of someone powerful or inspirational. It might be someone who constantly appears to be one step ahead of the competition. You could think of a specific person—someone famous or someone you know. You could even consider yourself.

The fact is that leadership may take various shapes and manifest itself in a variety of ways. Finding a real leader, on the other hand, is like finding a rare gem—it doesn't happen every day. People are frequently just concerned in what being a leader will do for them, selfish. Perhaps they desire more power, control, riches, acclaim, or a higher social standing. True leaders, on the other hand, are individuals who see leadership as a responsibility to others rather than a reward to themselves.

That's why my favourite definition of leadership is "an example for others to follow," which you can find in the dictionary. One of the most distinguishing characteristics of some of the finest leaders I've had the honour of knowing is that they live their lives in service to others. They understand that many around them look up to them and model their lives after them. As a result, these leaders seek to improve themselves. This is the unglamorous key to being a genuinely great leader—and to be honest, few individuals are prepared to take on such huge responsibility. This, I believe, is one of the major core reasons of the leadership gap that so many people in the corporate world are discussing these days.

But I'm not trying to be pessimistic or discourage you. I view the task of becoming a great leader as a tremendous opportunity. The finest leaders aren't always those who were given a particular "gift" from birth. They've decided to take on the huge responsibility of setting an example for others, and you can do the same. Anyone can do it. Anyone can choose to take up the mantle of leadership. Leadership is a skill that can be learned. That is the essence of "Intelligent, true, honest and real Leadership."

This book will offer you a road to become a leader if you genuinely want to grow as a leader and are okay with being "an example for others to follow." It's based on formal and informal research that I've done as an industrial psychologist and leadership coach over the years. I've worked with some of the finest corporate leaders—some well-known, some less so—and I've built a leadership technique that anybody can apply to become a genuinely great leader—and human being.

We'll go into great detail about true Leadership in the chapters that follow, but first I want to explore just what "great leadership" looks like.

Bosses certainly are not in short supply; real leaders are the elusive commodity. In the workplace and throughout life, each of us encounters leadership behaviours or organisational policies that we like or admire, and that we may try to adapt to our own business situations and lives. Conversely, we all know of, have seen, or have suffered firsthand from those bosses with not-so-admirable behaviours and policies that often are ineffective, counterproductive, and sometimes offensive. Of those people and their behaviours and policies we think, "Absolutely no way will I ever act that way!"

Follow-through on that statement, however, may be another matter. We are usually taught to boss, not to lead, and in many cases, bosses are the most prevalent role models. Rare today is the individual who inspires others with focus, trust, strategic know-how, and an instinct for knowing what's important, along with the ability to selflessly rally and mobilise his or her troops.

Many self-proclaimed and corporately chosen "leaders" are hardly more than bosses. Some people get a few hours of leadership training right away. Others believe they are in the position because they have a "natural talent" for it, while others claim they are just burdened with the obligations.

Unfortunately, regardless of whether the training is quick or extensive, the final product is still a boss, not a true leader.

I've worked in a number of industries for four decades, reporting to a variety of decision-makers, and I've seen a wide range of chief executives in action, both excellent and poor. I've also worked with philanderers, bigots, bullies, and egomaniacs with anger control issues as employers. Many were intelligent, but their actions jeopardised the success that true leadership might have brought to their businesses. One philanderer, for example, had an executive assistant whom he urged be promoted despite her ineptness. She had filed a sexual discrimination claim against him, it turned out. Another boss used workplace events as an excuse to dance with coworkers cheek to cheek. He also had a reputation for hanging out with his coworkers after hours, according to reports.

Consider how a true leader's attitude and conduct varies from that of a boss on a few important workplace issues:

Success in the workplace: A good leader concentrates on the long term and sets his or her firm for continued success. A manager is too preoccupied with the next quarter's bottom line to see the larger picture.

Employees: A leader is an advocate for the people who work for him or her. Employees are viewed as a means to an end by a manager.

A leader communicates directly with the board of directors, shareholders, customers, suppliers, and employees, taking the time to listen and answer in a thoughtful and modest manner that appreciates all of these individuals. A supervisor says nice things about his or her staff but is more concerned with his or her personal well-being.

Respect for others: A leader treats everyone with kindness and respect, regardless of their position. When it comes to executives, a boss is nice and charming, but when it comes to people he or she oversees, he or she is apathetic or demeaning.

Conflict resolution: A leader understands that conflict will inevitably arise at some point. He or she deals with it by directing it toward a positive outcome. A manager frequently causes conflict but fails to properly resolve it.

Managerial conduct: A leader will not tolerate insulting, rude, or verbally abusive behaviour from his or her subordinates. That type of conduct is often overlooked by bosses, who may even engage in it themselves.

Respecting an employee's personal life: A leader understands that workers have a private and personal life outside of work and understands the need of maintaining a work/life balance for well-being and productivity. A manager inundates his employees with numerous projects and unrealistic deadlines, then micromanages them.

Getting the job done: A leader strives to eliminate obstacles for his or her workers, offer the resources they need, and streamline procedures to make it simpler for others to do their tasks. A supervisor puts up obstacles that obstruct the job, result in unneeded extra labour, and cause unnecessary irritation.

We have all encountered the boss who takes the one-size-fits-all approach. That kind of disconnect and resulting disenfranchisement of employees happens all the time in today's multi-cultural, multi-racial, and multi-age workplace. That is, in part, why worker satisfaction is at an all-time low and why real leadership is so very important today. Rather than wield a cookie cutter, today's leaders must tailor their approach and style to fit the nuances of leading various generations and groups of people without compromising their ideals.

The newest members of the workforce are the Millennials, or so-called Generation Y, who present their own unique challenges. These are people born roughly between 1980 and 2000, and by 2014, they will be 58 million strong. Bosses likely call them the least respectful and most demanding generation yet. Real leaders, on the other hand, recognise that this generation brings tremendous value, skill, and insight to the workplace. Millennials require a different kind of real leadership, one that understands how to corral their energies.

Contrary to bosses' opinions, these "Gen-nexters" are passionate about their work, energetic, and committed, and they're tomorrow's leaders. They will improve their society's ingenuity, innovation, and competitiveness in an increasingly global marketplace. They're bright, industrious, and driven to succeed; they want to be challenged and given more regular feedback so they can improve. They're technologically savvy, cross-culturally aware, and committed to sustainability and diversity. Millennials are less trusting of corporate titans and politicians. They're also remarkably civic-minded and better equipped to be team-oriented, as a result of changes in our education system that now emphasize team-building and team activities.

The Millennials already boast some great leaders today. Mark Zuckerberg was a computer science student at Harvard University when he co-founded Facebook in 2004. The company revolutionized social networking. Larry Page and Sergey Brin co-founded Google. Google's head of marketing in the Middle East was Egyptian Wael Ghonim, whose Tweeting about the uprising in Egypt helped act as the catalyst to the revolution that overthrew President Hosni Mubarak. These are the real leaders who dare to have the vision and passion to bring new and radical ideas and approaches to life. Bill Gates and Paul Allen had similar visions and passions when they co-founded Microsoft decades ago.

Millennials gravitate toward organizations that assign them mentors, provide more frequent performance appraisals, give praise for a job well done at the successful conclusion of a project, and offer more flex-time. Non-tradition is the future in the workplace. Employers—big and small—must learn to evolve and embrace a new generation of workers or perish. Forget policies that aren't family-friendly. Penalizing parents for taking time to be with their kids doesn't cut it with this next generation. Neither does the silent treatment in the workplace.

Millennials want to work for companies that have an edge over others. They seek more growth opportunities and speedier advancement than their predecessors did. Thus, organizations that commit the necessary resources to construct their own internal talent engine will more often be selected by this group. It is critically important that businesses motivate the young workforce by closely connecting their jobs—and company success—to career development in a fully integrated way.

Millennials look at loyalty as a two-way street. Leaders today must exhibit a genuine interest in their employees. In a very real sense, they must look at them more as partners than traditional employees. Once a leader understands his people and what motivates them, she or he must adapt the workplace to take maximum advantage of their new way of thinking. This doesn't mean that the business must be run like a collective, but it does mean that they can't proceed in a business-as-usual manner.

The best leaders also genuinely connect with employees by showing their human side. Leadership, after all, is about relationships with others, and those relationships are essential to promote workplace culture and strengthen trust, which, in turn, increases productivity. Real leaders pay attention to employees' human needs, too.

Other important aspects of leading successfully in today's evolving workspaces include:

Adapting to differing demands or varied meetings that cross time zones. For example, one meeting may be an important special event celebrating a team's recent success, and the next meeting might be a very challenging encounter with investors, both involving participants across different time zones.

Maintaining what Simqu refers to as "calendar integrity"— doing what you say you'll do when you say you'll do it. Too many CEOs scratch meetings with employees at the last minute because the previous meeting ran longer than expected. That kind of disregard can quickly erode employee trust, because it conveys the strong message the employee is less important to the leader than other audiences.

Drafting your major messages yourself instead of turning the responsibility over to speechwriters or assistants. Once the message is established, at least in the form of ideas and a first draft, it may then be appropriate to hand it off to an expert or assistant to finalize.

Ensuring human resource staff are effective communicators and know how to work with employees off-site and on. Too many HR types don't know the difference and often are ineffective in working with employees off-site, especially when it comes to technology. IT staff need to be effective communicators, too, when remote or off-site workers are involved.

Being tech-savvy. Real leaders today—young, old, and in between—must learn to capitalize on all the communication means they have available, including social media such Twitter and Facebook, texting, Skype, and other teleconferencing methods. Leaders must take advantage of all this to stay in touch with employees, markets, communities, and key constituencies. As part of that, it is also essential to know the preferred forms of communication for immediate staff.

Ensuring that both remote and in-house employees receive the training they need to utilize these new technologies.

Being sure communications expectations and standards are clear and set up front. Don't leave response times to chance. Make certain that everyone is on the same page as to how he or she is required to communicate with the home office and the leader, how often, and what feedback is required.

As reflected in the outstanding actions of the individuals you have just read about, real leadership can and does bring about change. Real leadership is not always the fastest and shortest route, but it's definitely the most long-lasting and successful. Bosses can be transformed into leaders; like almost anyone else, they, too, can learn the right way to lead. A shift in attitude is the first step—from a domineering boss to a consensus-building leader.

If you strive to be a leader and not a boss, remember and subscribe to these values and practices:

Commit to driving fear out of your organisation.

Drive out other negative attitudes that undermine performance and morale.

Strengthen your corporate culture with discipline and compassion.

Believe in and build up your people.

Give clear assignments.

Be available when needed.

Listen attentively.

Display high integrity in everything you do.

You, too, can become a great leader by connecting with your employees. Some actions that can help entrench and enrich your leadership include:

Learning to shift gears quickly if necessary.

Doing what you say you will do when it comes to employees. If you promise to do something, follow through and follow up.

Not allowing others to draft your major messages. The voice of communication must be from the leader.

Being sure your staff members are effective communicators, too.

Being tech-savvy and not afraid to use technology to your advantage. That goes for social networks such as Facebook and Twitter, too.

Giving your employees and staff the tools and the training they need.

Setting specific standards for interaction/communication between employees, staff, and leaders.

Philanderers, racists, bullies, and egomaniacs with anger-management problems have no place in today's workplace, especially among the ranks of leaders. Not only do they undermine employee morale, but they also sabotage a business's success.

Real leaders must pay attention to the personal needs of their employees. Real leaders create a work environment—a climate or culture, if you will—that enables their associates to flourish.

Millennials bring unique and outstanding talents to the workplace. Real leaders must learn how to tap into those talents.

The 21st-century global marketplace requires an evolution of leadership strategies. With businesses operating 24/7 and across nations and the world, leaders must stay connected to their employees by every high-tech and traditional means possible, from social media to face-to-face visits.

Business leaders would do well to emulate the U.S. Marines' high standards of conduct, including traits such as the ability to adapt and the willingness to take risks, operate frugally, demonstrate courageous conviction, discipline, and inspire employees.

Today's leaders must be willing to take their businesses into uncharted waters in order to reap big rewards.

Bosses can learn to be leaders, and it starts with a willingness to shift one's attitude from domination to consensus-building and communication.

# CHAPTER 2:
# IS IT POSSIBLE TO BECOME A BETTER LEADER?

"Do you think that in order to be a great leader, you need to function in a way that contradicts with your own preferences?" This is one of the first questions I ask my clients when we begin working together. It's a bit of a trick question because you can correctly answer it in two ways. On the one hand, we all have enormous leadership potential, even if it is hidden deep within us. All we have to do now is nourish and grow these natural traits so they may emerge and lead our thoughts and actions.

However, even if great leadership potential exists inside us, who we are—our choices, conduct, and thought patterns—might not represent that grandeur. Less attractive characteristics and behaviours conceal and eclipse it. So, in order to become a truly great leader, we must transform. We need to alter our way of thinking, acting, and interacting. Essentially, we must transform into a new person, even if that person is a better version of ourselves.

This is the change paradox. It necessitates us not just becoming something new and different, but also becoming a deeper version of who we currently are.

I'm sure you've seen this contradiction firsthand as you've interacted with each of the elements of Intelligent Leadership. You could have had a profound connection with the power of opening up to yourself and others when we explored the vulnerability decision, for example. You may have even experienced the benefits of vulnerability in your own life. However, you may have been scared by this trait and avoided it for the most of your life. And you may have noticed that adding greater vulnerability to your life may help you tap into a whole new level of personal power and transformational potential.

Each aspect of Intelligent Leadership is both within and outside of you. It's something that has to be discovered and pursued. Both points of view are valid and essential. So, while you work to become an Intelligent Leader, I advise you to keep both in mind. Recognize that you can't improve as a leader—or as a human being—unless you change. At the same time, don't lose sight of the idea that your own potential greatness is within you. It's buried deep within you.

INTRODUCTION TO THE NEW

Regardless matter where you fall on the change conundrum, being an Intelligent Leader necessitates change. It necessitates the creation of something fresh. I've included activities and "igniter behaviours" throughout the book that you may use to help grow each component of Intelligent Leadership. I've kept these exercises broad because, in my experience, there's no such thing as a one-size-fits-all growth plan. My objective has been to offer you a clear understanding of these essential traits of outstanding leadership, as well as a set of tools to help you access and enhance them in yourself.

As we come to the end of our time together, I'd want to leave you with one more task. It's a straightforward method for manifesting anything new, whether it's a single trait or a larger goal for yourself. You can utilise all or any of the stages in the procedure. Whatever suits your needs.

The basic premise of the process is that in order to transform into something new, it's useful to have a vision of what that transformation may entail. This vision serves as your North Star, guiding you through the often arduous process of transformation. It clarifies the objective you're aiming for and provides you an idea of what you'll need to accomplish to get there.

Throughout my career, I've utilised this technique with thousands of individuals, as well as myself, and had consistently positive outcomes. There are six easy steps to follow:

Visualize: It's critical that you have a clear idea of who you want to be. This might be something particular, such as improving your communication skills. It might also be something more broad, such as improving your leadership skills. Whatever your idea, it's critical to take the time to sketch out as clearly as possible what this "new you" may look like. The more information you can give, the better. This image will not only offer you a target to aim for, but it will also implicitly connect you with the aspect of yourself that you want to emphasise.

Make a written and verbal record of your vision: It's critical to write out your vision after you've defined it, using as much detail as you can manage. This will help to solidify your vision and give you with a record to refer to as you progress through the process. After you've written out your vision, read it aloud. There's something powerful about expressing yourself. Words have a lot of power, especially when they are spoken. It has an effect on you when you hear your vision in your own voice. It adds to the realism of the situation. It holds you responsible.

Fill in the blanks: Pay attention to how you feel as you evaluate your vision, both written and spoken. Is there anything in particular that inspires you more than others? Are there any elements that make you feel uneasy or intimidated? Your emotional reactions might serve as an excellent indicator of where you stand in relation to your objective. These "differences" between who you are and who you aspire to be are crucial. They're the parts of your vision that may require the greatest attention in the future.

Make a list of everything you want to do: Make a list of the "gaps" between you and your vision once you've discovered them. Include some comments on why you included each item, as well as any emotional reactions you experienced when reviewing your vision.

Make a commitment to change: While this may appear to be a no-brainer, many individuals neglect it to their peril. The fact that you've made it this far in the process suggests that you're dedicated to change in some way. However, reiterating it has a significant effect. You may make a promise to yourself that you will dedicate yourself to realising the goal you've set for yourself and filling in all the gaps along the way.

Make an action plan: Now that you've defined and articulated your vision, identified the roadblocks to attaining it, and committed to overcoming them, it's time to put your strategy into action. The key, in my opinion, is simplicity. A brief introduction statement that explains what you are committing to in general should be included in action plans. They should also contain at least one action you want to take to close each gap you've discovered. You can include timeframes in any aspect of the plan, but the main aim is to provide an overview of the action actions you intend to take to reach your goal.

That's it: a straightforward method for realising a vision. Of course, if you discover that this method isn't for you, that's OK! Everyone approaches change in a unique way. I strongly advise you to seek out and do whatever actions are appropriate for you.

A GUIDED VISUALIZATION OF THE INTELLIGENT LEADER

As previously said, envisioning the objective is the first and most crucial stage in becoming anything new. In that spirit, I'd like to invite you to join me on a little adventure. To be a genuinely intelligent leader, I want to help you see what it would be like to be a thriving embodiment of all seven aspects of Intelligent Leadership. Of course, each person's expression of these aspects will be unique. These dimensions are designed to mirror the unique patterns that characterise each of our hearts, brains, and souls, much like light streaming through a prism. However, studying what a global Intelligent Leader may look like to help inspire your own personal visualisation is still worthwhile. By all means, go on to the next part if you'd prefer do it on your own without my help. Otherwise, let's get started.

The primary goal of intelligent leaders is firmly ingrained in them. They have a deep understanding of why they were here on this planet, and this self-awareness allows them the bravery to engage in great concepts. Their profound understanding of who they are allows them to express themselves in really distinctive ways that inspire others to think in new and different ways. They are forward-thinking individuals who recognise that they only have one life to have the greatest potential influence on others around them.

Strength is defined by intelligent leaders as more than the volume of their voice or the breadth of their authority. They understand that genuine power is demonstrated when they are willing to be vulnerable with themselves and others. Their candour astounds everyone around them, and it encourages others to follow in their footsteps. They understand that vulnerability is the key to change and the currency of strong, long-term relationships. They never forget that they can never accomplish anything without the trust and cooperation of others.

Leaders who have the most context are the most intelligent. They've developed the ability to rise beyond their own egoism by caring more about the many larger wholes of which they are a part. They have a remarkable level of maturity and dignity as a result of this. They believe they owe it to the task, their teammates, and themselves to give it their all in any scenario. Others gain confidence and space as a result of their perspective's breadth. People may take comfort in the knowledge that they are participating because they know they can always rely on them to make decisions that benefit the greatest number of people.

Intelligent leaders have a greater understanding of themselves than anybody else. They understand what special inherent abilities make them powerful, and they know how to put those abilities to the best possible advantage. They regard themselves—and everyone else—as constant works in progress in this light. They recognise that perfection is something that might be aspired at but never entirely realised. This allows them the self-assurance and confidence to confront even their most heinous defects. They don't flinch when they receive unfavourable comments, and they regard their faults and flaws as chances for personal development, allowing them to better serve others around them.

When it's time to act, and when it's time to wait, wise leaders know when to act. They are the ones that stand up and do what is necessary to take any situation ahead, while others are immobilised by fear, indifference, or a lack of caring. Their bravery stems from a profound sense of pride in themselves, but not the arrogant sort. They are proud of a job well done, especially when it is done in conjunction with others. Their actions are always marked by a genuine love for what they're doing, and they instil that same enthusiasm in others with whom they work. They see their profession as holy, and as a result, they carry out their duties with unwavering accuracy. They are the one that others can always depend on to do the right thing when it counts the most.

Leaders who are aware of the situation are awake. They are always aware of their environment and the circumstances in which they are acting. Even when others are letting their guard down, they stay focused on what matters most. They are unaffected by distractions because they recognise the importance of their time and focus. Their presence is irresistible. It enables people to feel grounded and keeps them accountable to a higher quality of care. Others may rely on them to always see things clearly since their motives are pure, and they are thereby receiving the most objective possible perspective on any given circumstance. They see things that others can't or won't see.

Intelligent leaders understand that work and life are both a never-ending riddle. Mistakes don't bother them; in fact, they seek them out because they realise that their capacity to course-correct is critical to their long-term success. They are eager to learn. They are looking for clarification. When change is required, they are willing to adapt. They feel at ease when they are not in their usual environment. They are issue solvers not because of any type of intellect or genius, but because they are the most eager to confront challenges, no matter how intractable they may appear to be.

I'm sure some aspects of this vision resonated to you, while others did not. There were probably some traits that you already have and others that might use some work. All of this is quite natural. We are complicated beings. Each of us has our own version of intelligent leadership. I invite you to recreate this picture in your own words. What would you look like if you mastered each of the seven dimensions? What would you do in that situation? Don't be scared to be detailed while you're writing. It is crucial to pay attention to the details.

You'll be well on your way to accomplishing your goals if you can develop a clear vision for yourself.

SHORT STORY

The protagonist, John Proctor, who has been jailed for being a witch, is presented with an existential predicament in one of the most pivotal sequences in Arthur Miller's classic drama The Crucible. His captors have offered him the option of signing a confession admitting that he is, in fact, a witch and being let free, or refusing to lie and facing execution. He decides to die with honour in what is arguably the most dramatic scene in the narrative. When his captors inquire as to why he has chosen such a terrible decision, he replies, "Because that is my name!" Because I don't have room in my life for another!" To him, his name, his legacy, is more important than his own life.

Proctor's pivotal choice encapsulates the essence of Intelligent Leadership. Of course, how you seek your personal growth as a leader and a human being isn't a life-or-death situation. However, the stakes seem to me to be comparable to those confronted by Proctor as he considered how his acts might damage his integrity and, ultimately, his soul. I believe that the type of leader you pick has far-reaching consequences. It isn't only about you, your own fortune, reputation, or celebrity. It all comes down to your legacy. It's all about how much of an influence you'll have on the world throughout your time here. It's all about your spirit. What will you think of your life when you're lying on your deathbed? Will you be able to relax? Will you be able to say that you done everything you could to make the world a better place?

Intelligent Leadership is all about answering this moral question. You may use all the techniques, skills, and strategies in the world, but unless you can connect with your inner sense of purpose and then organise your life around it, the effect you can have will be severely restricted. True greatness will evade you, and the success you achieve will be shallow and unimpressive.

This is where Intelligent Leadership comes in. It's also what makes it so unique and valuable. Leaders that are intelligent hold themselves to a high standard. They aren't satisfied with power or charisma. Character, honesty, and charity abound in intelligent leaders. They are aware that they are role models for everyone they come into contact with, whether personally or professionally.

We described leaders as role models who others aspire to emulate at the start of the book. They are the lights that lead us in the right direction. As we get to the end of the book, I'd want to encourage you to remember that basic concept once again. What type of role model would you like to set for your coworkers, friends, and children? Would you be proud of what mankind saw if they looked to you for examples of how a person should be or live?

At the end of the day, your response to this issue will decide your long-term leadership and life success.

# CHAPTER 3:
# LEADING WITH PASSION

Leadership is not about the size of someone's pay-check or the length of their resume; it is about passion, guts, and the willingness to give back. Too often, people confuse the need and desire to manage (boss) others or the craving to get rich with passion and guts. On the surface, these characteristics can appear similar. But closer examination quickly reveals how far apart they are when it comes to action, attitude, and reality. Bosses bully, whereas real leaders inspire by passion and guts, and rally those around them to follow and achieve greatness. Of course, we can't prove it scientifically, but it almost seems as if there's a "leadership make-up"—if not in the genes, then an alignment of certain traits that, if developed properly, can allow someone to flourish as a leader.

Passion in many forms surrounds us every day. But little of it translates into real business or community leadership that commits to helping companies, employees, and others so that everyone benefits from it. The brand of passion that infuses great leaders needs to be "fervor." It is an infectious lifestyle that includes living one's ideals, having a clear vision for the future, and possessing a mindset that enables the achievement of success in the face of adversity. For individuals who have found their passion, invariably life becomes more exciting, rewarding, and enjoyable, too. In the workplace, that passion translates into creation of a strong corporate culture that can help drive an organization's success in good times and bad. Look around you at those companies that have remained strong through the current recession. Somewhere in their make-up there is probably a passionate, real leader.

Passion is the best form of PR and fuels the perception by others that a leader is, indeed, just that. People want to know that their leaders—in government, business, church, sports, and elsewhere—fervently ascribe to what they say. They want to know that their leaders' views will not be easily swayed or vanish mysteriously when times get tough. People want to believe that the actions of their leaders are motivated by a strong sense of purpose and by values encased in passion. Above all, leaders must lead by example, teach others how to lead, be willing to always extend a helping hand to people in need, and always be humble and compassionate in how they approach life.

For some, passion is rooted in life's experiences. History is filled with stories about the kindling of a fervent flame—from the politician exposed to the plight of those less fortunate, to the college student encountering a professor who taps into something buried deep inside. Passion can be instilled at a young age, the result of parental modeling, and the discussions and decisions that shape a childhood environment. It is the same with other important lessons, such as the value of hard work and of not giving up in the face of adversity.

Leadership can be in the genes, too, waiting to be developed. For me, it started with the "family business." My grandfather, father, and uncles were strong community leaders and instilled in me that sense of purpose. My mother was a schoolteacher and hospital volunteer who introduced me to the importance of looking deeper within the individual and treating everyone with respect. With those foundations, I was able to watch, listen, and learn from those around me; build on experiences from supervisors, leaders, fellow workers, and beyond; and develop the concept of a real leader. I had great teachers, too—role models who made a big difference in my life and in the lives of others. Even without parents or grandparents, uncles, or siblings as role models, it is possible to harness your passions, learn how to lead others, and then excel as a real leader.

Positive passion and commitment surround us every day in the form of teachers who care, nurses who go the extra mile, pastors who reach out, neighbours who want to make their community a better place to live, and other individuals who deeply care and willingly volunteer. Too little of this passion, though, translates into real leadership committed to helping companies, employees, and communities come out winners.

Real leadership takes guts—not the kind of guts that it takes to charge into gunfire, but the kind that makes someone stand up for his or her ideals and confront the challenges on the figurative battlefields of corporate and personal life. In the world of sports, the commonly used motivational admonition "no pain, no gain," challenges athletes to reach a goal. In the military, soldiers say "no guts, no glory." In both arenas, as in business, maintaining a safe level of achievement is seldom the best option. This ability to make tough decisions despite the threat of alienating support can be learned and taught in business and in life.

In a recession or when a company is struggling, real leadership is not necessarily having the guts to lay off half your staff, either. It's more likely to be the intestinal fortitude for instituting painful, across-the-board pay cuts in order to retain an entire workforce through rocky economic times.

An important aspect of a real leader's inspiration is his or her ability to recognise need in the community and respond through charity and volunteerism. This is not a uniquely American concept or the sole purview of real leaders, but true leaders unquestionably manifest and exude the humility and gratitude inherent in giving back. Where a boss's attitude may be "I've got mine; now you get yours," a real leader says, "Let me share with you what I am fortunate enough to have."

Real leaders don't seek center stage; they seek success for others.

Finding your own passions and subsequent path to leadership in business and beyond requires a methodical approach punctuated by an abundance of patience and calm. We all dream of success, though everyone's dream differs. How we find our passions and accomplish our dreams depends on the effort we expend—not necessarily the money, but the work ethic. Each of us has to want it bad to achieve it. That's a part of what drives real leaders to find success. Too often in life, people—including the pseudo-leaders—"choke" under pressure because they're not passionate about what they are doing; they don't want it bad enough and are ill-prepared as a result.

To help you better recognize your own passions and develop your path to success, consider the following four-step approach:

**Assess**. Make a comprehensive list of what you do and don't enjoy doing now; how you do and don't like to spend your time, or what does and doesn't fascinate you. As part of that, inventory your current skills and those skills you would like to learn.

**Explore.** Ask others how they found their passions. Volunteer for a cause that interests you, take a paid or unpaid internship to learn about a business, or take a class on a topic that intrigues you.

**Experiment.** Take a risk by doing something new or outside your comfort zone. Seek out opportunities that offer new challenges.

**Measure.** Evaluate what you did, and how proficient you were at it. Would you benefit from more training, effort, or preparation? Was the experience invigorating? Most people can improve their skills in weaker areas even if they don't master every technique.

As I remind my students, your confidence will grow as you try new activities. I once took an acting class and studied opera. To my chagrin—or as I suspected—I had absolutely no talent in these areas. But, the experiences taught me to appreciate both arts and the skills possessed by performers. It is okay and healthy to feel strange or awkward when you're outside of your element and as you try new things. Don't be stymied by stereotypes or typecasting, either. We are all different; each of us has our own unique qualities, curiosities, and passions, and they will probably change through time.

Real leaders believe in themselves, their ideals, and their goals and aspirations. If they fall down, they get back up, and try and try again until they are successful.

Real leaders are resourceful; they know what questions to ask and of whom.

Real leaders have passion about what they do and how they do it, enabling them to tap into the needs, hopes, and dreams of those around them. These are leaders who make indelible impressions on others, in their words and in their actions.

Real leaders have the guts to stand up for their ideals and directly confront the challenges on the figurative battlefields of corporate and personal life. Playing it safe is seldom the best option—in business, on battlefields, or in sports.

Real leaders inspire by giving back to the community and sharing with others. Whereas a boss's attitude is "I've got mine; now you get yours," a real leader's attitude is "Let me share with you what I am fortunate to have."

Inspired leadership can be the fuel that helps others achieve things they might not otherwise accomplish on their own.

# CHAPTER 4:
# QUALITIES OF GREAT LEADERSHIP

What does being a leader mean? Is it a title conferred upon you by your employer or a quality you work hard to cultivate? The majority of us see the distinction between being a boss and being a leader. "Boss" is a title that is bestowed upon you, but "leader" is a title that you must earn. Leaders are down in the dirt working with their people to achieve a common objective, while bosses practise their golf putt in their offices as workers fight to keep the firm viable. Leadership has the power to create or ruin a company, and the good thing is that leadership abilities can be developed to make your company operate more efficiently.When employees discuss the distinctions between excellent and terrible leaders, they are referring to individuals who possess leadership skills against those who like to feel in control. Self-absorbed, egotistical, lazy, unpleasant, arrogant, and untrustworthy bosses are often despised. Honesty, support, trustworthiness, respect, and communication are characteristics of good managers who are classified as leaders. The distinctions are significant. In comparison to 18% of those with competent managers, 77% of those with terrible managers want to leave their employment within the following year. Vacancy is expensive, but a business culture built around enduring the whims of a poor manager is even more so.

To improve as a leader, you must assess your organization's goal and effectively communicate priorities to your staff. It will be obvious if you are not enthusiastic about what you are doing. Your enthusiasm will rub off on your coworkers, and they will follow your lead, even if you hold yourself to the same high standards as everyone else. But don't be too inflexible; reevaluate from time to time to see where modifications can and should be made to make the company's purpose more sustainable and realistic. In most cases, a leader will handle the larger duties and delegate the minor ones to workers, but it's vital to remember that whenever someone comes to you about a problem, everything matters.

You must cultivate the appropriate team for leadership to operate effectively. Hire individuals with talents that are distinct from your own and give them as much freedom as possible to accomplish their tasks. Leaders understand that the individuals recruited to perform the work were hired because they could do the job, and micromanaging is a symptom of a weak boss. Delegating authority to people who work for you allows you to concentrate on more important things. The core of teamwork is that everyone works together to achieve a common objective, everyone with their own set of abilities. When you've achieved your goal, make sure to give credit where credit is due. Leaders understand that no one rises to the top by themselves.

When you're confronted with the harsh reality that you're not viewed as a leader, it's a difficult pill to take. In business, the term "leader" is often thrown around carelessly. Do away with beliefs such as:

"I am a leader because I am a member of the executive team."

"I'm a performance manager, therefore leader, since I lead a team."

"Because I am a partner in my firm, I am a leader."

"I'm a leader because I'm the only one capable of doing this."

I'm sure you could be a leader in the sense of being good at what you do and leading a team to complete a task... Are you, however, a leader in the sense that you lead with example? Are you a role model for your colleagues and coworkers in terms of how you engage with them? Are you a leader when it comes to dealing with problems and concerns? When someone begs for assistance, are you a leader?

It's even stranger when you work for someone who is obviously a boss and tries to teach you into being a leader. They can recite what it takes to be a good leader in theory, and they can tell you where you need to improve in order to become one. Employees learn (also) by example, and how can you expect your people to learn from you if you aren't showing the traits of a leader?

A leader's and a boss's traits are vastly different. These distinctions have been shown in several memes and infographics. Workshops and character development seminars are also held by culture teams in organisations attempting to develop a workforce of leaders.

There are several more qualities that distinguish a boss from a leader. I've found the following to be the most relevant and true in my experience working with various managers:

A boss will tell you what to do, but a leader will demonstrate how to accomplish it.

It's a top-down approach. "Because I'm the boss, do it my way." A boss believes that they are always smarter than their employees and that they must have the final say. They desire complete control over everything that will make them appear attractive. A leader devotes time to training his or her followers. The world's smartest leaders employ people they believe are smarter than them. You invest in your people's learning and progress when you spend time educating them, and you foster long-term learning and self-reliance.

A boss speaks more than he or she listens; a leader listens more than he or she speaks.

A supervisor seldom cares what you think. They may pretend to listen to you at times, but their responses are frequently condescending or dictatorial. This also implies that they are more likely to offer you the answer rather than engaging in a conversation with you to discover a solution. And their responses are generally full of "how could you not have thought of that" sentiments that make you feel insignificant. A good leader would listen to you and collaborate with you to discover answers. A leader's emotional quotient (EQ) is generally what distinguishes him or her from a boss.

A boss is concerned with the problem; a leader is concerned with the solution.

A boss will criticise you for making a mistake and will frequently inform stakeholders of your error. A leader will try to figure out how the error occurred and then focus on finding a solution. In front of stakeholders, a leader will also accept responsibility for the error and emphasise on the 'we' rather than the 'you.'

A boss is driven by rivalry, but a leader is driven by passion and purpose.

A boss is competitive and may be deceitful at times. They want to be the greatest, even if it means preventing your achievement.

They are constantly striving to be the "boss" and are frequently envious of others' achievements. A leader wants you to be more successful than they are, and he or she enjoys and takes pride in the accomplishments of others.

A boss is a critic; a leader is a motivator.

A supervisor is more likely to focus on your flaws and find ways to criticise you or your job. A leader appreciates your efforts and abilities and frequently compliments you on them. When you're at your weakest, a leader will coach you to help you improve.

A boss is conceited; a leader is open to being exposed.

A supervisor is frequently too pleased of his or her accomplishments, boasting and justifying their actions. They feel that they are superior than others. A leader is willing to be open and honest with you. Their pride is in the group (team), not in their individual accomplishments.

A boss is the one who takes credit; a leader is the one who gives credit.

A leader wants to appear good in front of their stakeholders and claim credit for the team's efforts. Those who contributed to the success will be credited and rewarded by a leader. A leader sees achievement as a collective effort rather than an individual endeavour.

A leader is sympathetic, whereas a boss is domineering.

A boss's power is based on his or her ability to instill terror in his or her employees. You are forced to work by your boss. A leader establishes a safe environment and fosters passion and energy. A leader collaborates with you on the project.

Being an effective leader necessitates a complicated set of traits that I don't believe you can just learn. Compassion, humility, and empathy (among other qualities) must be developed through time into one's personality. I've worked with managers who have a clear understanding of what it takes to be a successful leader and have worked hard to show those traits. And that could work for a few weeks, but when they're under pressure, they revert to their original state, which is being a boss.

It's difficult to blame them. A lot depends on one's attitude and training as a result of their interactions with supervisors during their career.

It's odd because it's similar to parenting, or the youngster being subjected to a parenting style. Some children grow up to be precisely like their parents, while others intentionally strive to be the polar opposite of their parents. In the job, if you work with a toxic, micro-managing boss and understand the implications of how it makes you (as a staff member) feel and think, you either learn from that boss or do everything you can to become the polar opposite.

What really distinguishes a supervisor and a leader, in my opinion, is how they look after your well-being.

It's not even about how well you do or how successful you are in your position; they genuinely care about you. They're inquiring about your mental health, how you're dealing, and how you're feeling when they ask how you're doing. They are more concerned with your well-being than with getting the task done. I'm not saying that getting the work done isn't essential, but leaders recognise that we are all human beings who have ups and downs in life and react in different ways.

Bosses typically don't care about you as much as they care about the work. The only thing your bosses care about is that you finish the task. Even though I was suffering from a pounding migraine, my supervisor once insisted that I finish non-urgent tasks before taking sick leave. I even had a situation where I was at my wit's end and sought a couple of days of mental health leave, only to be informed that I could only take it two days later so that I could complete work for them. It wasn't even because I was the only one who could do it; it was just because they wanted me to.

Leaders recognise that their employees' health is critical to the success of their job. Employees who are happy, ambitious, and passionate who work in a healthy environment outperform those who are sad, scared, and furious and work in toxic, controlling, and unhealthy environments.

Employees who work under outstanding leaders are more likely to go above and above, and they are more likely to love their employment. The number one reason individuals remain or quit their employment, according to my discussions with people, is because of their bosses. This implies that some people may not enjoy what they do, but they adore their bosses, so they choose to stand out and remain loyal to them. Others may enjoy their jobs but despise their bosses, so they opt to quit. That should enough.

The distinctions between bosses and leaders are numerous. Supervisors and managers should evaluate their leadership styles on a regular basis to ensure that they are effectively leading their teams.

According to a recent Robert Half poll, 49 percent of professionals have abandoned a job because of a terrible boss.

Influence, motivate, and coach your team members and you'll begin to see that you are becoming a successful leader.

Delegating authority, being considerate to team members, enabling open communication, and having clear employee expectations are just a few of the essential techniques that every effective leader employs.

Although being promoted to a managerial position may appear to be a significant achievement, many professionals find the responsibilities to be more difficult than they anticipated. Being someone's employer does not automatically make you a good leader.

As more and more people leave excellent organisations due to one resolvable factor — terrible bosses – effective leadership is becoming increasingly crucial in the workplace. According to a recent poll conducted by the employment firm Robert Half, over half of all professionals surveyed (49%) had left a job due to a terrible boss.

"What are the attributes of a boss vs. a leader?" many professionals ponder this question whenever they move into management or supervisory jobs. We talked to leaders to find out the five major distinctions between the two.

Consider your own activities as you read the following comparisons to see which one you are.

Leaders have more clout than bosses.

According to Sue Andrews, a business and HR consultant at KIS Finance, the authority of a boss comes from their position, but the authority of a leader derives from their capacity to influence people.

"A boss's job is to make sure that people obey the laws of the business," Andrews told Business News Daily. "However, a leader will encourage others to think for themselves in order to reach the intended goals." "While a supervisor must issue instructions to tell others what to do, a leader may encourage others to choose the best path forward while encouraging them to reach their full potential."

Although employees only follow their leaders because they have to, Ken Gosnell, CEO of CEO Experience, noted that Corporate leaders may increase their influence by motivating their employees.

"Caring for your team, listening to their views and ideas, and expressing the 'why' behind the decisions and actions you do may help you build your influence," Gosnell added. "This is a secondary leadership step, but it makes all the difference, and people will follow you because they want to, not because they have to."

Leaders inspire, while bosses criticize. Leaders also give honest, positive criticisms too.

You shouldn't just describe a task and pass it over to your employee. A supervisor ensures you understand your task, whereas a leader supports and leads you through it, according to Christine Macdonald, director of The Hub Events.

"The most important distinction between a leader and a boss is that a successful leader inspires and motivates people," she explained.

Success necessitates passion; without a desire to finish tasks, employees will be less motivated to provide their best efforts. As their boss, you should inspire them by emphasising the importance of their task.

Leaders mentor and bosses discipline.

Employees are human, and they will make errors. How you handle mistakes reveals who you are as a manager. While many employers prefer to utilise a reward/punishment system to deter bad conduct, exceptional leaders recognise that people gain from praise and mentoring. If an employee excels in a particular field, that talent should be acknowledged and developed.

"The capacity to harness the skills of others to achieve a common objective is a fundamental part of leadership," Macdonald added.

It's critical to take notice of each employee's skills and shortcomings and mentor them individually. Rather of addressing skill gaps, focus on filling them by coaching people through their flaws and increasing their confidence in new areas.

Tasks are delegated by bosses; power is delegated by leaders.

A boss is laser-focused on their department's goals and adheres to strict process in order to achieve them. They prefer to micromanage and think in the short term. They delegate duties to their subordinates and think in the short term.

A boss has important objectives to fulfil, according to Christina J. Eisinger, executive coach and consultant at CJE Consulting, whereas a leader will define the long-term vision for the organisation and utilise it as "a major motivator."

"A manager achieves results by telling employees what to do and making sure they do it correctly," she explained. "A leader is concerned with doing what is right and is excellent at results by helping their team to find out what to do."

Andrews went on to say that leaders try to inspire people and promote commitment by establishing an example for others to follow. "They are at ease giving responsibility and refraining from micromanaging, preferring to watch others grow. They will influence people for the organization's overall advantage by utilising their outstanding communication and bargaining abilities."

Leaders are part of the team, whereas bosses are above it.

A boss, unlike a leader, does not take the time to get to know his or her staff. According to Eisinger, bosses see their team members as subordinates, whereas leaders see their team members as equal contributors and let go of the hierarchical divide.

It is critical to facilitate healthy interactions with your staff as a leader. Work with them to meet their requirements and foster an open-door culture.

"You'll be able to grasp how to convey your vision in a way that will truly connect with each person if you get to know your team better," Macdonald added. "This implies that you can tailor how you encourage individuals."

She went on to say that excellent leaders are sincere and devoted. You are a role model for your organisation. If you lack enthusiasm or motivation, your team is likely to suffer as well. Don't be scared to show your feelings and be genuine in order to connect with your coworkers.

How can you progress from being a boss to being a leader?

You may include a few essential tactics into your conduct to be a successful boss or leader. Three of these techniques, according to experts, include mindfulness, communication, and setting clear expectations for your staff.

According to Gosnell, you should treat your staff with care. A competent leader bases their decisions on the best interests of both the team and the organisation." Leaders who want to have an effect think about their people first "Gosnell stated. "They understand that acting in the best interests of their followers will provide excellent outcomes for both the followers and the organisation."

Leaders should listen to their teams and include effective communication into their plans. A listening leader, according to Gosnell, will hear ways to improve a company through the words of their staff.

"Those who listen to their team develop in influence and effect, while those who don't will suffer with disengaged personnel who won't listen," he continued. "A leader who wants to be heard should practise listening to his or her followers."

Whether you view yourself as a boss or a leader, the key to your success, according to Andrews, is that your employees regard you as fair in your dealings with them. Set clear, reasonable expectations for your employees and be consistent in your demeanour so they know what to expect from you.

"This is critical in the workplace since one of the most common sources of employee stress is not knowing what to anticipate from their boss," Andrews explained. "Staff will become uneasy if there are frequent shifts in emphasis and competing goals. Effective communication and a defined goal, on the other hand, will ensure that all teams are pulling in the same direction."

Team leaders are in charge of more than simply allocating work and keeping track of their staff. They are in charge of the team's overall success as well as the success of each individual team member. An successful team leader should be aware of each member's skills, limitations, and objectives in order to best use their abilities.

When defining a leader's key tasks, Eisinger devised a quick checklist for them to use:

Ascertain that the team has all they require to complete the task.

Provide employment that is both hard and fulfilling.

Be personable and available.

Hold one-on-one meetings with each direct report on a regular basis to discuss career advancement.

Performance should be measured.

Consistently provide feedback (both positive feedback and constructive criticism).

Don't worry if you haven't yet included all of these tasks into your work duties. Simply concentrate on improving and seeking input from your colleagues on how you can improve. Most good leaders, according to Eisinger, begin their careers as bosses but gradually develop into great leaders by using compassion and effective communication.

"It seems to be a natural transition point for people in the job I do as they first move into a supervisory role and build their leadership qualities," she added. "It's quite natural to have some of these 'boss' traits. However, in order to become a leader, it is important to identify one's particular obstacles and fight to overcome them."

Things would immediately improve, according to a mentor, if I altered my viewpoint while dealing with a tough employer and approached things in a way that made them feel like I'm contributing and setting them up for success. This means that if I inflate their ego and they win, I win as well. Sorry, but this wasn't the best advise. This demonstrated to me that bad behaviour is rewarded, and it is the employee's responsibility to alter and adapt. This isn't an all-or-nothing statement... I simply didn't believe it was a good fit for me. It was a band-aid for a serious problem, and it only works when things go smoothly.

So, here's some food for thought for those bosses out there who have employees. What kind of legacy do you truly want to leave? Professional connections aren't all that unlike from those you have outside of work. Regardless of your position, people are either for you or against you.

# CHAPTER 5:
# COMMUNICATION, SIMPLE YET DIFFICULT

One of the most crucial characteristics of a true leader is the ability to communicate effectively. True and honest communication, on the other hand, has quickly become a forgotten skill in today's digital era. Instead, high-tech devices and third-party mouthpieces have supplanted it, obstructing genuine contact and hastening communication's extinction. How many CEOs — or anybody else, for that matter – write for themselves, or schedule face-to-face meetings with subordinates, or even a phone call? How many CEOs genuinely listen to employees and managers when they meet with them? Today, the answer is a resounding no.

Face time may seem cumbersome in our global, plugged-in, tuned-in, digital world. Face-to-face meetings, as well as communiqués and statements made by genuine leaders, are established methods of effective communication.

We live in the "e-age" of communication, with software templates, texting and instant messaging technology, ghostwriters, public relations gurus, and downsizing experts all working to save time. Even multibillion-dollar transactions are reduced to back-and-forth messaging between executives, with attorneys and accountants left to iron out the specifics afterwards.

These days, a top-level executive may meet with high-level personnel on an ad hoc basis or on a regular basis to address corporate concerns. But how many of those encounters does he or she offer his or her entire attention to or show genuine interest in what is being said? There aren't many. When it comes to a CEO that genuinely writes his or her own messages, you'll have a hard time finding one. Again, there are many bosses, but only a few leaders.

Using all stand-in communication, as well as all digital—whether it's chat, Tweets, blogs, video conferencing, or third-party statements—is incorrect. Despite the fact that many senior executives have blogs and many more Tweet, few create their own material, whether it's blogs, greetings on Web pages, presentations, letters to the editor, or shareholder notes. To create their official documents and brief notes, today's leaders rely far too often on their in-house or outsourced public relations team, legal department, administrative assistants, or external consultants. According to a study of 750 executive bloggers conducted by the Financial Times in London, just two out of ten top corporate leaders really create their own blog entries.

The business world has forgotten the skill of communicating, blaming it on "I'm too busy" or "I'm too important."

Not every CEO agrees with the idea of "less talk, more action." Some people aspire for more, despite the fact that it frequently necessitates herculean, time-consuming efforts on their side. Blaise Simqu of Sage Publications is a CEO that communicates with his employees on a daily basis, no matter where they are. Simqu, who believes in modelling the conduct he wants from his staff, also understands the value of spending weekends with his family. That is the mark of a true leader. That wouldn't want to work for a boss who preaches and lives by balance for himself and his team?

Whether or not a CEO believes in genuine communication, it may and does provide significant outcomes. Any conflict can be managed and outcomes will be more effective if you interact and engage with colleagues, regardless of how combustible an issue or circumstance is.

True leaders are the authors of their own thinking. Sure, they might get some support from an assistant or a public relations professional to polish their work, but true leaders are responsible for their own thoughts, direction, approach, and attitude. They write their words down, plain and simple. Admiral Zumwalt may not have authored the final language for his "Z-grams," but you can guarantee he had a lot of say in the concepts, approaches, and attitudes reflected in each one.

Consider the following benefits for someone in a leadership position who writes their own communications:

CEOs are in charge of formulating and charting an organization's strategic path. Putting such thoughts down on paper or arranging them for personal contact helps them concentrate, reduces confusion and rework, gain others' trust, encourage followership, and enhance outcomes.

True leaders are also educators. Writing down your views first, then sharing them, soliciting comments, and debating alternate ideas is all part of the teaching process. Writing clarifies your vision while also increasing your leadership credibility. CEOs who create their big statements themselves are far more likely to galvanise stakeholders in ways that no ghostwriter can match.

Heroes, both past and present, abound in the business sector. These are people whose personal beliefs and visions weave the fabric of their missions, enabling their employees to be great leaders and their organisations to be immensely successful. These individuals are heroes who embody their ideals and are aware of what others say and do. They pay attention to their personnel, customers, and marketplaces.

We've all worked for or with the boss who is hard to reach, or heard about the boss who is tough to reach. Despite this, every genuine leader you've read about or will read about in these pages frequently mingles with, talks to, and learns from people around them. Real leaders do not shut themselves up in their "ivory towers," secluded from people around them. This communication fosters a sense of awareness and connection with the firm, its employees, and the community, all of which contribute to the company's success. For all levels of leadership, it should be normal operating practise.

Regularly engaging and networking with people in your organization—not only in your job strata—assists in the formation of long-term partnerships and gives critical short- and long-term feedback. If you're a CEO or executive, this entails spending time with your employees and customers. Outside of the office, it's important to be attentive and sensitive to people, and work and leisure environments might occasionally overlap.

Not every leader needs to travel the world, but all true leaders must listen and be approachable.

You may be the finest leader in the world—or at least believe you are—but genuine success will elude you until you can enlist the help of others.

True listening necessitates a keen awareness of what is going on in the workplace and in life. A leader is also willing to accept the personal and professional demands that these changes need.

If you're an aspiring leader who doubts the value of personal and real communication, do this easy experiment the next time you're out of the office: smile at the first few people you meet and see how they respond; odds are strong that the majority of people will smile back. Try the same experiment at work and see what happens. Begin connecting with individuals in your immediate vicinity on a personal level. It's probable that your connection with them will shift.

Although electronic communication is essential in today's corporate environment, consider limiting your use of Twitter and instant messaging (IMs) and avoiding relying solely on e-mail for all of your conversations. Instead, at your job, strive to approach projects and problem-solving with the same openness and desire to share that you displayed in your grin experiment. In an up-and-down economic situation, such personal connection may generate beneficial ideas and outcomes.

Almost everyone can recall an exchange of e-mails with someone at work or elsewhere that resulted in a misjudged cue, misinterpreted content, or a missed chance due to a misread cue, misunderstood content, or a missed opportunity. The e-mail "oops" might just be a misinterpreted punch line for a joke. However, if the e-mail conversation occurs in the workplace and the misunderstanding involves anything as significant as an insult or taking the wrong action that leads to a poor outcome, the ramifications can be considerably more serious.

Never let e-mail take the place of face-to-face conversation. Telephone conversations and face-to-face encounters cannot be replicated by e-mailing, texting, or Tweeting because they lack the personal and crucial subtleties as well as critical cognitive processes. Anyone who believes they can has not yet learnt the hard way.

Take use of the advantages of high-tech communications; just make sure you utilise them correctly and don't rely on them as your only means of "face-to-face" contact. For example, video conferencing may be a useful tool for project teams, or an e-mail or a Tweet might be useful for conveying a real-time confirmation. These communication tools are useful as a supplement, but they should not be utilised in place of more direct, human conversation.

Your conversation should be direct and personal, as well as genuine. Why should you, or any other leader, have to entrust speeches and other critical communications to speechwriters, public relations experts, or their assistants? The answer is that neither you nor they should. There's no purpose for it, especially now that there are so many computer applications to help with writing and planning. The iA Writer for iPad, for example, is a basic and straightforward word processor that can assist almost anybody put down their ideas, at least in outline or draught form.

Because it requires structure and growth of ideas, the writing process may be challenging for you as an unskilled writer. It is, nevertheless, a crucial step. When you plan strategy or decide policies as a leader or aspiring leader, if you create the content yourself, the end product is more focused, more thought out, clearer, and succinct. The personal connection develops employee trust and followership, which improves outcomes even more.

Why should true leaders continue to rely on physical ties and communications? As leaders, we must make advantage of every available tool to keep in contact with our workers, the community, our customers, and our markets. If we don't, the gap will become a serious danger to our business's success.

True leaders must go above and beyond to maintain ties with their teams and employees, or they risk losing touch. That isn't to say that leaders shouldn't use every other high-tech tool at their disposal to improve communication. This covers social media sites like Twitter and Facebook, as well as websites, e-mails, instant messaging, and texting, as well as more conventional channels like snail mail, paper handouts, and faxes. The aim of your communication strategy should not be to go "paperless" for the sake of going "paperless," but to build genuine and direct back-and-forth contact between leaders, their workers, their managers, and the community, and to do it right in order to stay competitive. There's no need to be short on communication in today's economy.

How could the people in your life communicate more efficiently and effectively by integrating electronic and conventional communication methods? What can you do in your personal life to improve your communication skills? What's keeping you from going forward and doing it?

Face-to-face contact not only establishes genuine connections, but it also allows you as a leader to have a deeper knowledge of what's going on in your workplace and in the marketplace. To offer your firm and workers a competitive edge, use face time to supplement comprehensive internet communication and more traditional forms such as faxes, printouts, and notes.

Set up a company Facebook page and a blog for your employees to discuss business and create ideas, and tweet the latest to keep connected with your employees and staff. Pay attention to what others have to say and be receptive to other points of view. Follow up with an e-mail, a note, or a bulletin board post, and then a face-to-face meeting to go through ideas and make sure everyone is up to date. All of these methods of communication may aid in the development of a true feeling of community and an atmosphere where people desire to collaborate. Remember that good leaders listen to all points of view, respect all parties, and then set out on a path to make a difference.

Face-to-face communication allows executives to engage with employees on a deeper level and have a greater understanding of what is going on in the workplace.

Social media, e-mails, texts, and instant messaging all have a role in the workplace, as long as they aren't the primary means of contact.

Confrontations or controversial topics are less explosive and simpler to achieve a consensus when a leader interacts and communicates with his or her team.

True leaders understand how to utilise humour to defuse and soothe situations.

Writing your own messaging aids in the clarification of your vision and strategic planning.

Real leaders must learn to pay attention to their workers, markets, and communities.

Connecting and networking with others, regardless of their professional status, can aid in the formation of long-term, strategic relationships.

# CHAPTER 6:

# A TRUE LEADER IS SELFLESS

True leaders aren't egomaniacs who want centre stage all the time, grab all the credit, and expect to be praised. Instead, they know when to take a step back and let others be acknowledged for their achievements. They are prepared to let others succeed in order for them to succeed themselves. Building a widespread culture of "leaders for tomorrow" in their businesses is a goal that genuine leaders set for themselves. "It is astonishing how much can be achieved if no one cares who gets the credit," is one of my favourite variations.

The best CEO is the one who has the foresight to choose good personnel to perform the job and the self-control to get out of their way while they do it.

Leaders typically assume authority and then move to the front of the room, above everyone. Depending on the success or failure of an activity, they are positioned to take the credit or the blame. When a problem arises, however, instead of accepting responsibility, the supervisors in charge cast the finger to someone else, further compounding employee and worker dissatisfaction and disillusionment. If a leader wants to get the most out of his or her employees and followers, being in the spotlight isn't always the greatest option.

The ideal job for a true leader—and the one with the best likelihood of success—is that of a facilitator. This means that as a true leader, you must train, educate, assist, and guide others before stepping aside to let them succeed. The true role of the leader is to prepare his or her soldiers for the work or goal at hand, then step back and let those troops—employees or others—do their tasks, achieve the specified objectives, and take credit (or, at the least, move forward with them arm in arm). A leader must also know how to mobilise his or her soldiers so that they comprehend and support the plan of action, engage in the vision, and respect the process in order to achieve success. Followers must comprehend the leader's vision, values, character, and beliefs, as well as have trust in his or her dedication and capacity to achieve his or her objectives.

Change is difficult to accomplish in a large corporation because few people enjoy it. With your courage, commitment, patience, and interpersonal abilities, you can get the wheels of change turning as a leader. Real leaders recognise the significance of beginning long-term reforms. They understand how to completely and properly prepare employees and staff for change, as well as how and when to step back so that people may embrace and own it. All of this is done while the leader is still in charge.

The first stage in the process for actual and aspiring leaders is to realise the necessity of preparing your team for upcoming changes. Your team—and you—will then succeed with the appropriate tools and training. Companies without true leadership today frequently fail to look beyond the short term and are unwilling to invest time and money in front-end preparation and training, resulting in a loss of back-end and bottom-line revenue. Employees frequently become frustrated, unhappy, and unproductive as a result of a lack of adequate training or an atmosphere in which to accomplish their tasks. Despite the current economy and tight labour market, some disgruntled employees may leave, leaving a firm with the pain, bother, and expense of replacing them.

It is contagious to be enthusiastic. Real leaders take use of this to their own and their company's benefit. The best leaders like not only had the proper concept about how to lead a team, but their passion for their objectives was contagious, resulting in excellent performance. Because their boss expected it of them, their team members wanted to perform the best job they could. From a business standpoint, that sort of zeal creates an almost irresistible force that drives employees and others to levels of success far beyond their initial objectives. Those objectives might be tiny and personal, or they can appear to be overwhelming and have far-reaching consequences. In any event, true leadership may be the difference between tremendous success and huge failure when it comes to achieving any objectives.

It all starts with true leadership, no matter how big the objective or how much change is necessary. Real leaders, after training their team, work toward attaining their goals one step at a time, building on the successes of those they lead.

Reading all of the leadership books in the world will not make you a true leader. It requires practise and experimenting with many solutions for various situations to learn how to lead. After all, no two employment circumstances will ever be precisely the same, and the world's fast changes will assure that this will continue.

Adversity and failure, though, give some of life's most rewarding experiences and lessons. The trick is to have a constructive perspective to life's difficult lessons and approach them with patience rather than panic. Then you emerge from challenging situations with more success and poise, and you learn crucial leadership skills along the way.

The King's Speech, which won the Academy Award for Best Picture, depicts the narrative of a king who is torn between two worlds. King George VI of England had to overcome a lifelong speech impediment and a cautious attitude in order to answer the call of leadership at the start of World War II. He had to learn to trust people, accept and face his flaws, and persist to achieve a goal.

Adversity of this nature may be a powerful motivation. If you've ever been asked at a job interview, "What is the largest setback or struggle you've ever encountered?" you've undoubtedly faced the problem of revealing a flaw at a time when you want to highlight your strengths. When everything else looks to be at its worst, many people are at their greatest and produce their finest work. History has shown us that leaders and individuals in general typically emerge stronger and more successful as a result of hardship. How a person responds to and recovers from major obstacles, adversity, or setbacks may reveal a lot about his or her actual talents and personality.

The most essential duty of a company's CEO is to foresee problems. Perhaps not to prevent it, but to prepare for it. Waiting till the crisis occurs is already a form of surrender. The organisation must be capable of foreseeing the storm, enduring it, and even being ahead of it. That is what innovation, or continuous regeneration, is all about. You can't avert a huge disaster, but you can develop a battle-ready organisation with strong morale that has also gone through a crisis, understands how to act, trusts itself, and can trust one another.

The ability to bounce back from misfortune is a skill that can't be taught. To grasp what adversity is and how important it is for life achievement, one must first experience it and strive to overcome it. Some of the most successful business executives in history have overcome hardship to emerge stronger, smarter, and with a greater sense of enthusiasm and desire to succeed. With their indomitable spirits, these losers-turned-winners are able to foster total trust among their employees and, as a result, have an inherent capacity to motivate a workforce to achieve new heights and perform their best job.

Credentials, a superior education, a solid upbringing, and even immaculate principles are insufficient to produce a great leader. Instead, learning the secrets to understanding what to do in each scenario requires the extra experience of suffering hardship—even failure—and persisting.

International leaders are dealing with a variety of problems throughout the world, ranging from economic and political to environmental and social. From Sacramento, California, to Washington, D.C., partisanship and rancour appear to outweigh compromise and consensus. Unfortunately, the lack of effective leadership is not confined to state legislatures or Congress; it also affects Wall Street and the nation's corporate boardrooms. Where are the true leaders who can effectively lead us through the current crises? Government and industry must produce a large number of leaders with the skills to balance long-term strategy with a willingness to solve issues quickly and teach as they go.

Businesses and organisations must make a conscious effort to train managers and lower-level employees how to become leaders in today's world. Presidents, CEOs, and other members of the executive team who take the time to teach, coach, and assist their subordinates and colleagues have a better chance of improving performance. Staff retention is also higher, which saves money. Furthermore, nurturing young talent guarantees that the firm will have a smooth transition when a leader steps down.

The military is usually a great training ground for developing leadership qualities that may be applied throughout one's life and career. Working in a confined environment, whether at sea or as part of a squadron or platoon, requires you and your team to handle problems swiftly and successfully, because lives are often on the line. Team members are far more likely to succeed if they are empowered, understand the significance of taking the lead to address difficulties, appreciate the value of clarity of purpose, and believe in their own skills. All of this helps to develop leadership abilities.

There's a reason why General Electric CEO John F. "Jack" Welch and his successor, Jeff Immelt, are frequently referenced in leadership, management, and training publications. They both feel that part of their personal leadership role is to groom tomorrow's leaders. Welch, in fact, nurtured Immelt, his successor at GE.

GE Crotonville, currently known as the John F. Welch Leadership Development Center, has been dedicated to developing the company's future leaders for decades. It is now an international leadership training institution based in Ossining, New York, that annually welcomes thousands of workers from GE's global businesses. Executive courses in leadership, innovation, strategy, and manager development are among the options for future leaders.

New manager leadership courses that emphasise development, business effect, and external attention.

Courses in essential skills like as recruiting, presentations, team development, and project management are available.

Executive briefings, change management, and integration are examples of customer programmes.

90 percent of GE's top 600 leaders have been promoted from inside the business, demonstrating the program's effectiveness. They've got to be doing something right, right?

Many organisations make the error of thinking that developing leadership requires engaging top-tier consulting firms or employing up-and-comers from prestigious universities. Both are money draining methods in both good and bad economic times; more importantly, neither option fits the bill.

I had recently joined a major business and had ambitions to go up the corporate ladder. As a motivated new employee, I was eager to take advantage of the company's prospects. So I inquired about the company's initiatives for identifying and developing future leaders from inside. My clearly startled and perplexed employer answered by stating that the company's current approach was to hire outside expertise. Spending institutional resources on leadership development, he claimed, would produce discontent in the C-suite, raise controversy since "winners and losers" would emerge, and amount to preferential treatment in an otherwise equal atmosphere. I didn't last long at the firm. Any company, big or small, that prefers to hire from outside instead of grooming and promoting from within (intra-organizational leadership development) is doomed to fail in the long run.

Leadership development should not be limited to the top echelons of businesses. Companies and their CEOs must create an organisational culture that fosters the development of future leaders from the bottom up, teaching not only leadership qualities but also a thorough grasp of company strategy and culture. This method aids in the delivery of long-term benefits and real innovation. Internally produced executives who understand the company strategy and culture, as well as the personnel and network to expedite job delivery and the internal credibility to promote smart change, should be at the heart of a diverse organisation.

I believe it is vital to adopt a process of identifying fundamental leadership qualities for each managerial job inside a company, regardless of size. It's thus crucial to identify and assess each manager's real capabilities inside a company, as well as compare them to the stated leadership competencies for each management job. This method will provide a "gap analysis" that will highlight important areas of competency and leadership development for tomorrow's leaders. It is simpler to build leadership development programmes that reinforce and expand the abilities that managers need to improve after these gaps have been recognised.

There is no lack of "leaders-in-waiting" in today's workplace, fresh talent expecting to be discovered, mentored, pushed, and developed by senior management. Instead, there is a scarcity of firms ready to commit to leadership mentorship. Too few companies understand the competitive advantage that may be gained by developing this conduit or pipeline of future leaders. Real leaders understand that the more high-quality ideas that arise from all levels of a company, the more likely it is that better judgments will be made. In today's top leadership businesses, the flattening of corporate leadership is taking place, where leadership is distributed across the organisation and at all levels rather than concentrated in the hands of a few at the top.

To do so, however, organisations must invest in leadership development, and those that do so will be the most successful.

The University of Southern California's meteoric rise as an academic powerhouse over the last two decades is an excellent illustration of what can be accomplished with the appropriate infrastructure—or leadership pipeline—in place. Instead of recruiting elite academics, well-known military commanders, or staunch business titans like GE, Boeing, IBM, Four Seasons, or Ritz-Carlton, the school's administration chose to develop future leaders from the bottom up. Up-and-coming executives would already be familiar with the company—USC—as well as its strategy and culture.

Today's firms, large and small, might benefit from emulating the US military's leadership pipeline, particularly the US Marines. Of course, yelling drill sergeants, running large distances in double time, and practising tactical weaponry would not be included in future corporate leadership training. However, military concepts such as strategic thinking, learning by doing, executing complicated plans, metaphorical tactical weapon usage, and so on might be beneficial. Junior officers learn to think strategically, design and execute complicated plans, manage and inspire enlisted troops, be responsible for costly equipment, and remain calm under duress. Regular counselling, critiquing, challenging, and correcting of performance by senior leaders, as well as learning by doing, are all important aspects of training. The Marines are a great example of how to achieve the aims of having workers that know the competitors and the playing field, understand the objectives, are well-trained to attain those objectives, and can do them swiftly and efficiently.

One approach for a firm to stand out from the competition and attract top people is to have the appropriate type of built-in, coordinated leadership training—the correct leadership pipeline. Consider the following good strategies for producing tomorrow's leaders. If you use them, your business will most likely be more successful:

Strengthen your bench press. Success in athletics, like in business, necessitates a lineup of starters and backups who can be called upon when needed. This depth of skill helps the team win titles and earn new business.

Develop leaders at all levels of the company. Most businesses are large and complicated, necessitating skill development across the board. An organization's culture and brand are sustained through a pool of developing leaders.

Create a variety of opportunities for younger employees to take on more responsibility.

Executives and other leaders should be obliged to devote significant effort to discovering and developing talent at all levels of the company. Top executives who routinely give learning chances for young managers are also more successful.

Enhance the human resources department. Its duties should include overseeing an in-house leadership development curriculum, which is necessary for the company to offer value. A cohesive, systematic approach to leadership development is considerably more successful than disparate, sporadic attempts by different departments.

Develop the moral fibre, principles, and ethical standards that today's leaders sorely lack. When prospective leaders are faced with real-world situations that need them to make decisions, they acquire valuable lessons. When core values and ethical standards are taught early in a profession, they are more easily imprinted.

Leadership development is not just the duty of enterprises and businesses outside of schools and institutions. Many community and corporate organisations, as well as regional organisations, schools, and universities, provide educational opportunities for leaders. Local chambers of commerce are frequently linked with programmes that are best positioned to discover and nurture future leaders. Leadership San Francisco and Stanley K. Lacy's Executive Leadership Program Opportunity Indianapolis are two that I have participated in.

These types of leadership programmes cover a wide range of themes and subjects, depending on the complexity and economic health of the community or region. Despite this, the programmes all have significant leadership development aims in common, such as:

Getting a deeper understanding of current community concerns and needs.

Getting to know corporate and civic leaders who have had a significant impact on the community's development.

Obtaining the knowledge and resources necessary to become effective community change agents.

Identifying each student's unique interest, forming connections with others, and widening perspectives.

Establishing a large network of community connections, friends, and mentors.

Increasing volunteer and board engagement in local not-for-profit organisations.

The majority of programmes last between eight and eleven months. Typically, each new class will spend a day learning about the community from experienced leaders. They will also learn about relevant community issues, focus on each class member's own leadership abilities, and explore possibilities for improvement. Many programmes start with a retreat (usually a two-day event) that includes things like leadership training activities.

Leaders who have blazed a way in the field of leadership will give talks.

Personal leadership styles are investigated.

Discussions and discoveries on people's and viewpoints' variety.

Members of the class participate in interactive learning.

These leadership training may be beneficial to both employers and employees. Graduates of the programme are more valuable to their employers as knowledgeable future leaders. The leadership pipeline of a firm is expanded, and programme alumni are better mentors to their coworkers. As a bonus, the business's brand is enhanced by its workers' involvement with other well-known companies, particularly if the company supports programmes or events as part of the leadership training.

Across the country, more companies and industry executives should consider participating in chamber-endorsed leadership initiatives. These programmes are important to communities, and they function with your company's best interests in mind: to develop genuine leaders for your company's and community's futures.

Potential leaders may be found in a variety of places, including the often-overlooked arts. Nothing is impossible when labour, devotion, and pleasure come together to form passion. Music, the arts, and theatre require a high level of imagination, as well as discipline, dedication, and passion—all qualities that are frequently absent in today's floundering enterprises.

In today's competitive market, successful businesses must realise the necessity of grooming tomorrow's leaders, as they will decide the future success of their organisations. The most essential job of a CEO is to put in place a mechanism for identifying and grooming future leaders for the firm, as well as to train and mentor existing future leaders. A robust leadership pipeline ensures that a successful firm is passed down from generation to generation.

The following are some questions to consider. There are no right or incorrect answers, and they aren't meant to test your knowledge. Instead, it is anticipated that considering the responses would aid you in understanding the role and advantages of fostering future leaders as an aspiring leader:

Is there any formal leadership training for current employees at your company?

What more could be done to help future leaders develop their leadership skills?

Is your firm reliant on hiring outsiders to fill senior positions? If that's the case, can you explain why? Is there anything you can do to make the process go more smoothly?

Is it necessary for a company to hire "superstars" in order to maintain a high-performing portfolio, or can it achieve continuous top performance by utilising the capabilities of its current employees?

What are some of the ways that a company may enhance its line staff' performance?

Consider how you performed at work. Are you utilising all of your abilities? If not, why not, and what would it take for your organisation or its leadership to help you achieve your highest level of performance?

True leadership is something that can be learnt. Real and wannabe leaders alike must cultivate and develop the following qualities:

Humility.

Quiet self-assurance (rather than arrogance).

Preparation for virtually any circumstance that may arise.

Toughness on all levels: physical, mental, and moral.

Personal gain trumps commitment to the team.

Belief in the larger good and causes above one's own self-interest, as well as a readiness to forego personal gain for the better good.

A facilitator—a trainer, instructor, and supporter who leads others and then steps aside—is the best position for a true leader—the job with the best possibility of success.

Adversity may be a powerful motivator and educator. Some of the most successful business executives have overcome hardship, failed, and returned stronger, wiser, and with a greater desire to succeed.

Because organisations and their CEOs must establish an organisational culture that nurtures future leaders from the bottom up, leadership learning should occur at all levels of a corporation.

True leaders cultivate a large and diverse pool of future leaders inside their organisations.

The United States Marine Corps may teach businesses how to develop a leadership development programme. Junior officers are taught to think strategically, design and execute complicated plans, manage and encourage enlisted troops, be accountable for expensive equipment, and remain calm under pressure by the Marines. Regular counselling, critiquing, challenging, and correcting of younger officers' performance by senior leaders are also important aspects of training.

Outside and community leadership initiatives may benefit both employers and workers. Not only do the programmes build a leadership pipeline, but they also help programme alumni become better mentors to their employees.

# CHAPTER 7:
# CHARACTER AND INTEGRITY

True leadership is a 24-hour job that incorporates everything a leader stands for and accomplishes both personally and publicly. A leader must not only possess all the qualities of Effective Leadership, but also be a pillar of integrity and character. Being a true leader is a complex and difficult task that only the most dedicated individuals can master.

In today's competitive economy, any breach of character or lapse in integrity, whether genuine or perceived by others, might endanger a company's or an individual's success. A single event may cast a pall over an otherwise brilliant career and severely harm an organization's or individual's reputation, obliterating years of image-building and shattering the brand as a result. Consider how Tiger Woods' personal and professional reputations were harmed as a result of his well publicised infidelities with his wife. Remember how Toyota's enviable image was damaged by enormous, seemingly never-ending automobile recalls? What is the public's opinion of our government's integrity after watching one U.S. Rep. after Rep. is involved in a series of ethical scandals? Remember how badly British Petroleum was panned in the aftermath of the Deepwater Horizon accident and the massive oil leak in the Gulf of Mexico? Each has had their reputations seriously damaged, maybe beyond repair in certain circumstances.

Individuals, businesses, and enterprises throughout history have made mistakes and learned harsh lessons by failing to live up to the task of sustaining strong character and sterling integrity at some point. Some people and businesses recover, while others do not. Those who do recover face a lengthy and hard journey that often leaves them falling short of previous achievements. That is why it is critical for organisations, whether large and small, to safeguard their brand by protecting and developing the character and integrity of not just their leaders, but also all of their workers.

Top leaders are frequently derailled by even minor blunders. Paul Levy of Harvard Medical School was a much-desired true leader with perfect character, great ethics, and all-around abilities. However, he temporarily lost sight of the significance of embodying the leadership precepts and was accused of having an improper relationship with an employee. It makes no difference what kind of relationship was involved or if it was appropriate or not. Levy's men lost faith in him as a commander, and he resigned from his position.

One indiscretion is all it takes to ruin — or at the very least raise questions about — people's faith in you. You must never lose sight of or contact with integrity, honesty, and excellent character as a true leader. If you have any concerns about anything, don't do it; if you have doubts, chances are others will as well. Above all, never think of yourself as superior to others around you. You are solely responsible for yourself and your actions. "It takes many good actions to create a good reputation, but only one evil deed to destroy it," Benjamin Franklin stated more than 200 years ago.

The foundation of leadership development is character. Those in positions of leadership must have a strong moral standing and unquestionable ethics. After all, it is these leaders' responsibility to teach, influence, and form people who work with, for, and around them. No one wants to lose such a high-ranking job due to skewed ethics and morality.

We presently place a great value on well-known people and celebrities as a culture. These are today's "heroes," if you will, despite the fact that they frequently break no moral or ethical rules. We don't expect them to. However, if our heroes—whose conduct we often model—fail, we may likely fail as well. True heroes still exist, albeit they are sometimes lesser recognised, who exhibit excellent ethics and values, as well as integrity, strength, and humility, for all of us. It is critical for organisations and people to keep these lesser-known but real heroes and their accomplishments in mind.

"Character, character, and character are the top three criteria of a successful leader." "I know there are people who would refer to former President Bill Clinton and argue that despite having relationships in the White House, he did wonderful things as president, therefore character is unimportant. Despite this oddity, the public places a high value on leaders' honesty....

People are characterised by their behaviour in the face of hardship and difficulty. When things go wrong and the pressure rises, a person's character is put to the test. Whether in business, athletics, or coping with more personal concerns, a person's character is put to the test when things go wrong and the pressure mounts. The leaders I admire the most are those who, in the face of adversity, remained cool, focused, and unselfish, and chose the correct path rather than the easy or popular path. 'When no one is watching, character does the right thing.' Too many individuals believe that getting by is the only thing that is right, and getting caught is the only thing that is bad.

Character is not the same as integrity. Every business, like every individual, has its own unique personality and culture. Each of us is defined by our character, which includes our values, where our moral compass points, and how we respond to ethical dilemmas. It determines whether we do the correct thing when no one is looking, as well as what values and ideas we pass on to future generations. In a nutshell, it's who we are and what we may become as true leaders.

Integrity is doing what you say you're going to do and admitting it to yourself and others if you can't. "The final effect of someone with outstanding character is integrity." "Show me someone of good character, who is completely honest, who follows the rules (even if he or she doesn't agree with them), and who refuses to put their own interests before of others...and I will show you someone who acts with tremendous integrity."

True leaders, like the rest of us, make errors. The difference between true leaders and bosses is that, while real leaders strive hard to avoid making errors, they are quick to accept their failures and move on. Bosses either deny or point the finger at someone else when mistakes are made. And woe to the employee who makes a blunder; a supervisor is unlikely to forget about it—ever.

Despite the fact that truth is the guidepost and the objective, a true leader cannot and should not always reveal the full truth. If a firm is preparing to introduce a new product or execute a new branding strategy, revealing the launch date or specifics of the plan and its implementation might endanger the venture's success. If a leader is skilled at communicating, his or her team will understand the delicate nature of the issue and the need of keeping "classified" information confidential. However, in order to maintain secrecy, it's preferable to be vague about launch dates and other sensitive information. When a CEO is interviewed on an issue that, if he or she were completely honest, may give the competitor an advantage, ambiguity can be useful. In a situation like this, honesty is crucial, yet full disclosure would be a betrayal of trust.

Above everything else, honesty is crucial. "In my experience, being upfront with the reporter about the reason why you are unable to fully discuss the subject is a solid approach," he adds. "Experienced reporters can notice an attempt to evade or obfuscate fast, and if they suspect someone is lying or being deceitful, they usually find a way to indicate in the article that the subject was less than cooperative/truthful.... In the end, being honest and up up about not being able to address the subject may not gain you any instant brownie points with the reporter, but it will earn you respect and trust in the long run."

To be a true leader, you must be willing to be a trailblazer and a change agent. That involves moving outside of your comfort zone to help your company succeed. Real leaders will follow a course of action because they really believe in it, even if it contradicts common opinion, after carefully evaluating the benefits and drawbacks. They'll also try to clear the way for their team's victory.

True leaders must acknowledge the loss of trust and commit to rebuilding and reconstruction. A resolve to try something new at least once a week, if not every day, may make a big impact. Hiring CEOs on the basis of their moral fibre, in addition to the normal criteria that executive search firms and boards of directors mutually establish, is the true leaders' prescription for restoring employee trust. Companies must scrutinise potential candidates with the same conviction and high standards as White House Cabinet officers and Supreme Court justices, and ensure that the CEO's behaviour, as well as his or her performance on the job and off, is more closely monitored and objectively evaluated by the organization's board of directors.

Using President Ronald Reagan's trademark phrase, "trust but verify," which comes from a Russian proverb. We've all seen far too many examples of boards abandoning their governance responsibilities and, as a result, their responsibilities as corporate "watchdogs." Today's board practise of determining CEO remuneration by "benchmarking" other CEOs' wages and perks rather than their company's performance is far too common.

Realigning pay plans to close the gap between CEOs and lower-level employees. Companies must demand that CEOs act as real leaders who genuinely appreciate their workers as partners and exhibit openness. CEOs may achieve this aim by taking regular acts that reflect their dedication to their staff over time.

Having no hidden motives, providing as much information as possible, and recognising that there is no such thing as a private conversation. To put it another way, businesses must provide the same information to all of its stakeholders and never say anything they don't want repeated.

Accepting responsibility for their faults and alerting others about them right away.

In today's workplace, core values such as honour, service, and cooperation are all too often lacking. If the phrases seem familiar, it's because they're leadership characteristics taught by the United States Marine Corps—that top-tier training I mentioned before. Add the basic concept of honesty to those values. They give great leaders credibility when they work together. Honesty extends well beyond what is spoken. Individuals' and bosses' or leaders' nonverbal cues are frequently as significant as their spoken ones. In their acts, true leaders are modest and sympathetic, but their words are firm. When speaking with you, true leaders will look you in the eyes; they are equally as steadfast in their pursuit of their objectives and convictions.

Use the truth or consequences test to see if you're telling the truth. Take note the next time someone speaks to you—especially if he or she is giving you directions—and see if they look you in the eyes. If this is not the case, one must question if he or she is telling the truth. Genuine leaders are forthright and uncompromising.

Make sure that any nonverbal indications you provide or receive are consistent with your fundamental values and the principles of true leadership. If they aren't, figure out why and strive hard to bring them together. You'll be more consistent in your words and actions, and people who contact with you will enjoy it—whether they know it or not.

Too many people write unhelpful performance reports because they aren't completely honest. Whenever a performance review is superficial, spiteful, or somewhere in between, it was most likely prepared by someone who thinks like a boss rather than a leader. A true leader will invest time in honest and open communication with his or her staff, and will not jeopardise his or her character or integrity by creating or "fudging" a critical performance assessment. After all, if a leader is doing his or her job of teaching and mentoring tomorrow's leaders, a performance review will be candid and constructive, providing the employee with clear direction.

There are far too many grades given to pupils who have not earned them. There are far too many testimonials made by persons who should not have been used as a reference. Once again, it is genuine leaders' open and honest communication that provides the vital lessons that help others achieve.

The capacity of a leader to win the trust of his or her personnel is critical to the success of any team or business. Despite this, research after study shows that loyalty is eroding all around us. To achieve robust economic recovery, trust must be restored. Real leaders understand the importance of rebuilding trust and devote the time and resources necessary to do it. Is there a lack of trust in your workplace? If so, what's the reasoning behind it? What can you do to increase workplace trust?

Rebuilding trust necessitates genuine leadership actions. Those in positions of leadership can take concrete actions to assist create trust, such as:

Recognizing and applauding others' achievements and triumphs.

Management and leaders are chosen based on their talents, ethics, and morality.

Investing in fail-safes to ensure that management meets or exceeds expectations.

Putting in place performance-based pay.

Employees should be treated with honesty, openness, and candour.

Taking responsibility for your faults rather than blaming others.

Many effective leaders may improve their outcomes by learning how to build stronger alliances, coalitions, partnerships, and relationships with others. How confident are you in your ability to enlist mass support for the causes that matter to you? What can you do to enhance that skill? Are you committed enough to such projects? What more can you do to fortify key connections and win universal acceptance?

Consider how essential it is to believe in what you're doing and how you're doing it the next time you're in a position to rally the troops. How can you expect others to believe in you if you don't believe in yourself and your mission?

What do you do when you fail at something or don't meet someone's expectations, whether they're yours or someone else's? Do you immediately move on, or do you pause, analyse the situation, identify any errors made by you or others, consider what might have been done better to enhance the outcome, and then proceed? We're all expected to learn from our errors, whether we're real leaders or not. Even when great outcomes are achieved, it is critical to examine the processes and actions that led to that achievement and to consider what may have been done differently to improve the outcome even more.

How might enduring or recovering from hardship assist mould a young leader's skill set? What can you take away from your triumphs and failures? What are some of the errors you've made in the past when it comes to leadership? Write them down, then consider how you could have handled the situation better to minimise or mitigate the error's negative consequences.

To solidify your own true leadership, trust in yourself and what you can do, then follow the credo of service over self, empowerment over control, and serving rather than being served with zeal. Instead of pursuing "atta lads" for yourself, go after them for your team members and their projects.

Pay attention to the thoughts, ideas, and opinions of others around you as well. They are quite helpful in establishing your own viewpoint. In that spirit, surround yourself with people who excel in areas where you lack expertise, and don't recruit "yes" men or "yes" women; instead, be confident in your own judgment—your gut instincts. It's wonderful to use actionable data before making judgments, but keep in mind that having too much data may reduce the necessity for your smart judgement.

Also, be cautious while employing new employees. People who are usually negative, circumventers, or who may try to disrupt team efforts should be avoided. If you find yourself working with someone like this despite your best efforts, have the courage—true leadership—to confess your error and rectify it.

The foundation of leadership development is character.

True leaders face difficult issues and difficulties front on, and they are not hesitant to speak up for their principles and ideas, no matter how unpopular they may be. Be wary of any executive who avoids controversy. When properly directed, conflict may be a powerful force for good.

Honesty and integrity are fundamental qualities of true leaders.

Others are inspired to follow leaders who believe in themselves and their goals.

Employee trust must be rebuilt by true leaders. To do so, you'll need a dedication to employing people based on their skills; fair and equal remuneration for everyone; an open and honest attitude; and, if you make a mistake, admitting up and moving on.

# CHAPTER 8:
# TO LEAD, YOU NEED TO UNDERSTAND YOURSELF FIRST

You've undoubtedly heard the term "Know thyself" if you've ever taken an introductory philosophy class or spent any time reading one of the many personal development books available today. Socrates popularised this ancient Greek proverb, which he built upon, according to his pupil Plato, to develop the famous remark "An unexamined life is not worth living."

This is not to boring you with a review of Western philosophy's history, but rather to introduce you to the type of inquiry that is at the heart of Intelligent Leadership. If you want to grow as a leader, which includes growing as a person, you must analyse yourself as thoroughly as possible. You need to know what motivates you, what gets in the way of your success, and what hidden talents you may have.

As we stated in the opening, understanding what you're looking at is crucial to ensuring that your self-inquiry yields meaningful, long-term outcomes. Are you primarily interested in achievements, abilities, and behaviours (the part of the iceberg that is visible—the outer core)? Or are you looking into your inner core's deeper structures, which include your character, values, thought processes, and beliefs? The Intelligent

Leadership approach is centred on expanding your understanding of all of these aspects of yourself.

I'd like you to think about who you are when no one else is looking. In what ways do you demonstrate a strong sense of self? Are there any areas where you lack character? This may seem like a strange exercise to you, but it's the key to unlocking your leadership potential.

I'll offer you with some criteria for evaluating your character to assist you with your query. Character, in my opinion, consists of six aspects, which I've listed below. They are the map of your personality, and they are an important part of your inner core. Consider how strongly you demonstrate each element as you read through them, and where you could have opportunity to improve. Examine the data to see if any trends emerge.

Courage

It's simple to envision a mythological hero fighting a monster or rescuing someone in peril when you think about courage. While the core of the term may inspire this grandiose notion of bravery, the real definition of courage is generally far more nuanced. Courage, as a character characteristic, is simply the willingness to put oneself in harm's way for a larger good— whether it's speaking truth to power, risking your reputation by making a difficult decision, or doing the "right" thing when there's a lot of pressure to do something other. Courage isn't about being fearless; it's about being willing to act on your convictions despite your fears.

Where do you stand on the subject of bravery? How eager are you to put yourself in harm's way for others or for the greater good?

Loyalty

I don't mean "blind" commitment to a person regardless of their behaviour when I say "loyalty." Loyalty is the glue that binds our relationships, as well as the fabric of our communities and organisations, together. Loyalty is what permits us to stick by one another through good times and bad, even when it isn't convenient. Loyalty is a two-way commitment that must work both above and below. The devotion you exhibit to your superiors is directed upward, and it is tempered by the idea that the superiors are lawful and ethical. The obligation of leaders to care for their people is referred to as "downward" loyalty. It's called "loyalty to the troops," and it's just as important as upward loyalty.

Is it vital to you to be loyal? Do you find that you are dedicated to people, even when it is tough, and that you follow through on your commitments?

Diligence

In essence, diligence is the recognition that there are no quick cuts to worthy accomplishments. Anyone who settles for the fastest, simplest, and shortest path to a result is certain to be disappointed. If you're ready to put in the effort to ensure that you've done all possible to achieve, you'll have unshakeable confidence. Due to their preparation for the likelihood of a rocky road, diligent leaders are far more resilient in the face of setbacks, and they are able to navigate forward despite obstacles. They don't have the nagging sensation that they could have done more or made better choices. Diligence gives your character a solid foundation that allows you to stay grounded among the turbulence of the world around you.

How conscientious are you in your life? Do you resist cutting corners in order to ensure that you've completed tasks correctly?

Modesty

Leaders have a lot of confidence, which makes humility one of the most essential aspects of developing a powerful personality. At its heart, modesty is about staying within one's means. It is the polar opposite of aggression, arrogance, and presumption. The most effective leaders understand that they are not "too big to fail," and they are willing to consider other viewpoints in order to better themselves and their organisations. Fiscal and operational restrictions are protections rather than hindrances for the humble leader. Modesty also helps you maintain emotional equilibrium. You may build a calmer self-acceptance in the midst of adversity if you realise that your most haughty tendencies are based on a need for attention.

Would you describe yourself as modest? Are you able to control your ambitions?

Honesty

When it comes to character, it may appear that honesty is a no-brainer, but the fact is that being honest is more difficult than one may imagine. It's sometimes simpler to compromise the truth in the name of expediency, profit, or personal development, especially when you're under a lot of pressure. The finest leaders are willing to pass up agreements that would need dishonesty in order to succeed. A lesser profit earned via honesty is worth more than a larger profit earned through deception. Dishonesty accumulates over time—padded expense accounts, cut tax returns, coming late and departing early, or theft of corporate property—creating a poisonous atmosphere in yourself and your team. A mature and honest leader, on the other hand, fosters an honest and open workplace.

What value do you place on honesty? Do you ever compromise the truth in order to obtain something?

Gratitude

While expressing thank you and letting others know they are appreciated are essential expressions of appreciation, I'm talking about something more when it comes to character. Gratitude stems from the realisation that we will experience highs and lows in our life and in every activity we undertake. Higher is preferable, just like batting average, but the rare strikeout may also be a learning lesson. In reality, it is the lows that keep us grounded and allow us to enjoy the highs much more. Gratitude for what comes your way will come naturally if you retain a bird's-eye view of your life and don't feel entitled to achievement.

In your own life, how thankful are you? Are you able to have a broad picture perspective on your triumphs and accomplishments?

Did you see any trends emerge as you studied and considered these six aspects of character? In my work with all sorts of leaders, I've found that contemplating character is one of the most illuminating activities. It helps to build a picture of how much inner strength you have in the face of adversity, and it gives you some very practical strategies to enhance these essential aspects of your personality.

Character is essential, but it's only one element of the deep core equation. Your values are the next important aspect of your inner core.

It's critical to begin exploring why you do the things you do if you want to understand yourself. This is where your values enter the picture. The term "values" can refer to a variety of things. Consider a specific value such as "family," "success," or "recognition."

The lens through which we perceive the world is our values, especially our deeply held ones. Every important decision we make is influenced by them. Some of our values may be personal ideals that we've developed. Others were implanted in us as a result of our parents' or society's influence. Whether we are aware of our values or not, they influence our every action and, to a large extent, decide our fate.

Despite this, few of us, in my experience, take the time to properly figure out what our values are. We have a tendency to go through life acting on ideals that we have never given any thought to. And this can frequently result in issues.

For example, I've worked with executives who appear to struggle with establishing good personal ties, which can hold them back both emotionally and professionally. After some investigation into their unconscious values, it became clear that they were primarily motivated by a strong desire for success and achievement, which was a valuable asset in many ways but, if left unchecked, would frequently conflict with their desire to improve their interactions and bonds with others. We weren't able to discover this disparity and so begin to change the balance in their lives until we mapped their value set.

So, in the spirit of self-exploration, let's delve further into your own value matrix. There are many various types of values that a person may have, but for the sake of Intelligent Leadership, we'll concentrate on what's known as "ultimate" values. Ultimate values, such as recognition or security, are vital to who we are and serve as the foundation for our more immediate priorities, such as money or family.

The underlying drivers of who we are and how we act are our values, and they have a big impact on our leadership style. Everyone of us has a unique set of values. Others are motivated by recognition or compassion, while others are motivated by power or tradition. Understanding your personal hierarchy of values is crucial to figuring out what makes you tick.

Here are a few techniques to help you figure out which values are more important to you. Your values, for starters, are frequently mirrored in your attitudes and hobbies. Pay attention to the pleasant sensations you have connected with each of the 10 ultimate ideals as you explore them. You may have a natural gravitation toward knowledge and dislike to security. Perhaps it's the aesthetics that piques your curiosity.

Consider how you spend your time in the previous week, month, or year to assist you figure out your values hierarchy. What activities have taken up the majority of your time, and what values do they reflect? Do you spend a lot of time at the workplace late? Could this be a sign that you value commerce and want to ensure that your business is profitable? Alternatively, it might be a reflection of your desire to be acknowledged by your supervisor or peers as someone who goes above and beyond to achieve success.

Are you shocked by the findings when you build your own list? Is your value system consistent with how you see yourself? Now is a perfect moment to share your values hierarchy with the support network you defined in the introduction, if you're brave enough. Inquire about if they agree with your evaluation of your values or whether they have a different viewpoint.

Discrepancies between your values hierarchy and how others see you are common. These differences are normal and provide you the opportunity to push yourself farther. Why do you think you placed "altruism" higher on your list than your network did, for example?

Character problems are frequently the cause of the disparity between what you believe you value and what others see as your values. Remember that character is a reflection of your moral strength—your willingness to behave in ways that are controversial or go against your own self-interest or ego. If you have certain character flaws, it may frequently affect how your values manifest themselves in your life.

Please be patient with yourself as you continue to discover your character and beliefs. We're all flawed, and the goal of the Intelligent Leadership approach is to find methods to better ourselves and make a larger difference in the world. I'd think you're either a flawless human being or not being diligent enough if you breezed through this task with little to no effort. I'll leave it up to you to decide which one is most plausible.

Our self-concept and beliefs are the final elements of our inner core. These are the ways in which our inner character and values are manifested in our basic actions and talents. Unlike your personality and values, which are often unconscious, your self-concept and beliefs are more likely to be conscious aspects of yourself.

Simply said, self-concept is how you see yourself. Do you think yourself yourself as a success or a failure? Is it better to be a leader or a follower? Is it better to be an extrovert or an introvert? Your self-concept will have a big impact on the type of person and leader the world encounters. And many of your leadership shortcomings may be linked back to a problem with your self-concept.

If you believe you are a victim of circumstance, for example, you may find yourself unable to deal with difficult events on a regular basis. You'll constantly feel helpless to rise above your problems and overcome them. However, regardless of your position, if you perceive yourself as a problem solver, you will be more likely to accept responsibility for yourself and people around you.

The finest leaders have a strong sense of self-worth. This might be the product of a naturally optimistic view on life, which may have originated from your familial or cultural upbringing, or it can be the consequence of continual reinforcement of that positive image based on previous accomplishments. If you've consistently surmounted hurdles in your life, you'll be more confident in your ability to manage future challenges. You've proven it to yourself, and in the process, you've strengthened your self-concept.

This is excellent news. It indicates that you can improve your self-concept even if it isn't as positive as you'd like it to be. Like the other aspects of your inner core, your self-concept is flexible. You may literally change your self-concept for the better by self-examination and practise.

I'll give you activities to help you develop a stronger and more positive self-concept as we go through the seven aspects of Intelligent Leadership. Each dimension will shed fresh insight on your current self-concept while also providing opportunities for it to grow and expand.

Your self-concept is inextricably linked to your beliefs. When you hear the word "believe," it usually refers to thoughts or beliefs that are founded on faith or intuition rather than proof or truth. This might be a belief in some sort of higher power or in people's innate goodness.

However, when I say "beliefs," I mean something slightly different. The concepts that we know to be true through repeated experience are the beliefs that I'm seeking for. For example, we may feel that humans are naturally nice since we've witnessed acts of generosity and kindness from others throughout our life. As a result, our actions in the world are shaped by this firmly held conviction. Because we think that deep down inside everyone is goodness, it gives us a feeling of hope and limitless possibilities in how we judge and connect with people.

Another example I often see in leaders is an unspoken assumption that individuals are incapable of true change. They believe that individuals are who they are and can't truly change in major ways, even if they never confess it or even realise it's part of their worldview. This might be the result of years of accepting things as they are, or it could be the result of early childhood traumas. In any event, they are undermining their own efforts to change by holding this mindset, because they don't believe it is feasible.

In this context, beliefs have a significant impact on the sort of person we are and the leadership potential we possess. One of Intelligent Leadership's aims is to help you deconstruct your beliefs, figure out which ones are holding you back, and then start building new belief systems that will help you grow as a leader and a human being.

# CHAPTER 9:
# REAL LEADERSHIP REQUIRES EMOTIONAL INTELLIGENCE

Most of us would acknowledge that our emotions have an impact on our performance in certain aspects of our lives, and that this is both natural and good. In sports, we witness the influence of emotion as we try to psyche out our opponents or motivate our teams. In all sports, "attitude"—mood and emotion—is crucial.

But what if you have a profession that requires a high level of logic? Emotions clearly cannot and should not play a part in highly logical and analytical judgments. In a landmark research, psychologist Alice Isen discovered that even ostensibly logical people like doctors change their thoughts and decisions based on their mood. In a study with radiologists, she discovered that when they were given a little present, their diagnosis were both faster and more accurate (presumably mildly elevating their moods).

People who strive to conceal their emotions end up retaining less information, according to social scientist Roy Baumeister. Emotional repression appears to consume energy and attention that may otherwise be spent listening to and processing information.

This isn't to say that we should always be filled with emotion. Instead, we may use techniques that do not entail repressing our feelings to comprehend the underlying facts as well as the emotional component of the event. Emotional reappraisal is one such technique, in which we examine the difficulties but try to reframe them in a more productive and adaptable manner. We see the circumstance as a problem that has to be solved, or we try to learn something from it.

Please don't get us wrong. Managers that are emotionally savvy don't just plaster a grin on their face every morning and strive to have a happy attitude for the remainder of the day. Emotionally intelligent people, on the other hand, aim to avoid Pollyanna-like positive reactions to everything all of the time. Dealing with problems—or avoiding them—in this manner is ineffective. An emotionally intelligent manager is one who is aware of his or her emotions and then uses them as a springboard to a successful and productive end.

Managers and leaders frequently withhold some sorts of information from their employees or attempt to hide their emotions in order to protect themselves or others. We act as if everything is OK when it isn't; we act as if we aren't concerned when we are.

Organizations have a reputation for attempting to regulate emotions, particularly the exhibition and expression of emotion. Employees in many service-oriented occupations are trained to hide their emotions and put on a cheerful front. This is the concept of "emotional work," which was initially popularised by sociologist Arlie Hochschild. People attempt to exhibit the emotions that their employer requires in a variety of ways. One method is by surface acting, which is when you act as if you are feeling one way but don't express the actual, underlying emotion. Deep acting entails attempting to modify your present emotion to match the intended one. Surface acting, as well as emotional labour, has been related to performance fatigue, job turnover, and other difficulties, as you might anticipate.

Emotional repression in the workplace may take many different forms. We do not display strong emotions or feelings that the organisation or group deems improper in a process known as normalising emotion. The kind of emotions that people are instructed not to express at work may surprise you. Consider your personal experiences with organisational life. What emotions do you see people displaying, and what feelings do you see people displaying infrequently?

If you mentioned that rage is a suppressed and covered-up feeling at work, that may be true at your place of business, but it is not true in general. Anger was the most common emotion conveyed to the individual who caused it in one workplace survey. In fact, according to this survey, 53 percent of respondents voiced their displeasure. The sensation of delight was the least often expressed emotion at work, with just 19 percent of participants claiming to have expressed it.

These findings appear to be paradoxical at first glance. Anger is a strong, unpleasant feeling that people attempt to hide and conceal, whereas pleasure is a positive emotion that appears to be more acceptable to express. However, organisational emotional standards demand that joy must be expressed in a non-professional manner. After all, this is work, and we shouldn't be having this much fun at work. Anger, on the other hand, is a display of power and authority, a way of letting people know who's in charge. We're not suggesting that this is how we should conduct our professional life. We think that expressing delight is a vital component of the emotional intelligence manager's toolkit, and that we should celebrate our accomplishments more frequently and encourage one another to replicate them.

Although these attempts to mask our feelings are deliberate, they may not be very effective. According to Ekman's study on facial expressions and lying, monitoring pauses in a person's speech, speech mistakes, and fleeting emotional displays might help you detect a liar. In the workplace, our urge to shield emotions or engage in strictly rational pursuits can lead to poor decision-making and a distrustful environment.

You may attempt to be the tough-guy loner type in management—a John Wayne of organisational effectiveness—and it will work on occasion. However, this isn't always the case. Some individuals will read your sentiments and emotions the majority of the time, while all people will read them occasionally.

Whether we like it or not, our emotions have an influence on us and others. Simply said, no decision is taken without feeling. As we previously said, neurologist Damasio believes that rational thought is impossible without emotion.

Western philosophers and academics frequently make the mistake of separating thought and body. We've constructed a split-personality image of ourselves as logical creatures (with reasoning, or ideas) battling irrational urges (originating in our bodies, or emotions). Even now, many individuals appear to have this viewpoint. Emotion is viewed as untrustworthy, illogical, and undesirable urges that regress us to a lower evolutionary level. Consider this excerpt from a magazine article promoting the question, "What's Your EQ?":

Perhaps the most important area of disagreement between various approaches to the issue of emotional intelligence and ours is illustrated in this excerpt. We realise that emotions make us genuinely human and underpin logic, therefore they must be welcomed, embraced, understood, and put to good use in our approach.

Although we will teach you the significance of methods such as mood regulation and management, we will stress the entire experience of emotion rather than shutting it out or justifying it. It implies that as a manager, a team member, or an individual contributor, there will be occasions when you will be hurt, deeply harmed. However, if it doesn't hurt at times, you're probably not making emotionally intelligent—or effective—decisions.

Pleasant or good emotions encourage us to investigate our surroundings, widen our thinking, and expand our behavioural repertoire. Positive mood encourages us to try new things. It aids in the discovery of new connections and the generation of fresh and innovative solutions to issues.

We are affected by positive emotions in different ways. Happiness, for example, drives us to play or connect with others; smiling and laughing, on the other hand, communicates to others that we are pleasant and approachable. Positive emotions strengthen social ties and strengthen social networks in this way.

Positive emotions protect us against bad events and feelings as well. People recover more rapidly from the physiological impact of a stressful event if they are made to view a film that elicits strong negative feelings and then merely instructed to smile afterward.

Negative thinking has recently gotten a bad rap. Negative emotions, on the other hand, are essential because they may improve thinking in extremely practical and beneficial ways. The following are some of the impacts of a bad mood or emotion on thinking:

Increasing the clarity of concentration

Allowing for a more thorough examination of details

Motivating a more efficient error-finding process

Negative emotions make us want to modify what we're doing or what we're thinking about. They focus our attention and awareness, and they encourage us to take certain actions.

Negative emotions are more intensely felt as compared to good emotions, and this phenomena may have an evolutionary cause. An injury or an assault has higher survival costs than the potential advantages of discovering something intriguing in the wild. Negative emotions that warn the possibility of danger must thus be treated with greater caution, and if they are felt more intensely than happy emotions, we are less likely to wind up on a predator's dinner table.

We all enjoy good emotions and acknowledge their benefits to our health and well-being, but so-called negative emotions like fear, rage, and contempt should also hold a special place in our hearts. There is a moment to be at peace—to feel pleasant feelings—and a time to be at war—to feel negative emotions. It is not the goal of management to prevent conflict and keep everyone happy all of the time. Management is primarily about efficiency, which necessitates a wide variety of emotions.

Emotions arise for a variety of causes, but they are always part of a sequence that progresses from low to high intensity. If the event or thought that triggered an emotion continues or increases, the feeling is likely to get stronger as well. Emotions aren't something that happens at random. Each emotion has its own set of moves, similar to a chess game. All you need to know is whatever piece you hold and what the rules are for that piece.

How can you aspire to grow more emotionally intelligent if emotional intelligence is simply that, a type of intelligence? After all, according to many studies, your IQ is what it is and remains pretty constant throughout your life. Is your emotional intelligence quotient in the same boat?

We don't know for sure, but we do know that humans can learn new talents and gain knowledge. Emotional intelligence, as evaluated by the MSCEIT, is greater in middle-aged individuals than in young ones, for example. We believe that the talents that make up emotional intelligence may be enhanced. After all, one of the goals of this book is to assist you in further developing your emotional understanding and abilities. Knowledge is a good place to start when it comes to developing skills in this area. To really develop these abilities, you must go beyond merely reading this book and put them into practise. We'll provide you the information you need to improve your emotional intelligence abilities, and we'll help you take action. The remainder, and most importantly, the most important portion of growth, is up to you.

Emotions and thought are inextricably linked. We all know that emotions may help us think at times and can also get in the way of our job at other times. Being able to match the mood to the circumstance is an important part of becoming an emotionally aware manager. Getting into the appropriate frame of mind leads to a helpful mindset, which is one of the cornerstones to innovative thinking, empathy, and vision.

Sure, for some people, sentiments don't help them think better, but they do make it worse. It occurs to all of us from time to time. However, for other people, it occurs frequently. That's because people have either an angry or a cheerful temperament, and their "natural" or baseline emotion is either anger or pleasure (or some other feeling).

Feelings and thoughts are inextricably linked. The question isn't simply, "When does emotion help with thinking?" but rather, "When does emotion help with thinking?" The question is also, which emotions help us think more clearly? In this chapter, we'll show you how emotions affect our thinking and how to get into the proper attitude for each situation—the mood that will help you achieve your goal.

Emotions have an impact on how we think. Emotion is required for thinking to take place. These are the two core concepts of emotional intelligence. Let's take a deeper look at how various emotions guide attention and initiate thought.

Happiness permits us to come up with fresh ideas, think in new ways, and perceive new possibilities. Having dreams and seeing them come true is what happiness is all about.

# CHAPTER 10:
# NEW STRATEGIES FOR 21STH CENTURY LEADERSHIP

THE MANAGEMENT APPROACH OF COMMAND AND CONTROL has grown more unviable in recent years. Globalization, new technology, and shifts in how businesses produce value and engage with consumers have all diminished the effectiveness of a top-down, directive leadership style. What will fill the void left by that model? The way leaders manage communication inside their organizations—that is, how they handle the flow of information to, from, and among their employees—is part of the solution. Traditional business communication must give way to a more dynamic, intelligent approach. Most importantly, it must be a conversational process.

While working on a recent study project about the state of corporate communication in the twenty-first century, we came to that conclusion. We interviewed professional communicators as well as senior leaders from a variety of organizations—large and small, blue chip and start-up, for-profit and charity, domestic and international—over the course of more than two years. We've spoken with almost 150 folks from over 100 firms thus far. Participants in our study highlighted their attempts to "have a dialogue" with their employees or their desire to "advance the discourse" inside their organisations, both implicitly and explicitly. We created a leadership paradigm called "organisational dialogue" based on the ideas and examples obtained from this research.

Top-down, one-way communication between leaders and their staff is no longer effective or even feasible.

When leaders engage in meaningful communication with the people who work for and with them, they gain significantly greater engagement and credibility. A conversation is an open and honest exchange of ideas and information with a purpose, either implicit or explicit.

The discussion in the workplace reflects a new reality: Employees have discovered a public voice, thanks in part to digital and social technology. Whether their managers like it or not, they'll utilise it.

The good news for CEOs is that employees may promote a firm in a more fascinating and appealing way than any visible public relations effort.

We've discovered that today's smart leaders interact with their staff in a style that more closely resembles a normal one-on-one conversation than a sequence of orders from on high. Additionally, they establish procedures and create cultural norms that promote a conversational mindset throughout their businesses. One of the most significant advantages of this strategy is that it allows a large or expanding firm to operate as if it were a tiny one. Leaders may preserve or regain some of the traits that allow start-ups to beat more established competitors by communicating with workers rather than just issuing instructions. These qualities include operational flexibility, high levels of employee engagement, and tight strategic alignment.

We identified four components of organisational conversation that match the key characteristics of interpersonal communication when constructing our model: intimacy, interaction, inclusiveness, and intentionality. Leaders that use conversation-based strategies to fuel their companies don't have to cross all four of these i's. These components, however, tend to reinforce one another, as we observed in our research. They eventually come together to form a single integrated process.

Getting Closer to Intimacy

Personal communication develops when the parties remain physically and symbolically near to one another. Similarly, organisational dialogue necessitates leaders minimising the institutional, attitudinal, and occasionally physical gaps that normally divide them from their people. Those in positions of decision-making power seek and gain the confidence (and hence the attentive attention) of those who work under them in situations where conversational closeness dominates. They do it by learning to listen to individuals at all levels of the company and by learning to talk directly and genuinely with employees. It is not always possible for leaders and employees to be in close proximity. It's also not necessary. The importance of mental or emotional closeness cannot be overstated. Conversationally competent executives come down from their corporate thrones and take on the task of engaging with their employees in a human and open manner.

Organizational dialogue differs from more traditional types of business communication because of its closeness. It focuses on a bottom-up interchange of ideas rather than a top-down delivery of information. It has a less formal and more informal tone. And it's more about asking and answering questions than issuing and receiving commands.

Conversational closeness may take several forms, including building trust, listening attentively, and becoming personal.

Developing trust

There can be no intimacy if there is no trust. For all intents and purposes, the opposite is also true. No one will engage in a genuine debate with someone who appears to have a hidden goal or a hostile demeanour, and any conversation between two individuals will be gratifying and substantive only if each person can accept the other at face value.

However, trust is difficult to come by. Employees have found it increasingly difficult to place their faith in their leaders, who will only earn it if they are honest and forthright. This may entail discussing subjects that are taboo, such as confidential financial information.

Listening attentively

When it comes to corporate dialogue, leaders who take it seriously know when to shut up and listen. Attending to what others say is one of the few activities that improves conversational closeness. True attention conveys a feeling of respect for individuals of all grades and roles, as well as a sense of curiosity and even humility.

When he was CEO and chairman of Cinergy, Duke Energy's president and CEO, James E. Rogers, began a series of "listening sessions" (which later merged with Duke). He held three-hour seminars with groups of 90 to 100 managers, inviting them to raise any important concerns. He acquired knowledge from these talks that might have otherwise gone unnoticed. He learned of an issue with unequal remuneration from a group of supervisors during one session, for example. "Do you have any idea how long that would have taken to come up through the organisation?" he inquires. He could immediately order his HR staff to find a solution after hearing directly from individuals affected by the situation.

Getting down to business

Rogers asked individuals to voice their complaints about the firm as well as provide criticism on his personal performance. At one point, he requested staff to rate him on a scale of A to F. The anonymous findings were instantly displayed on a screen for anyone to see. Although his grades were typically high, only about half of his coworkers were prepared to award him an A. He took the remarks to heart and began repeating the workout on a regular basis. He began to ask open-ended questions on his performance as well. Surprisingly, he discovered that "internal communication" was the area in which the majority of participants thought he could improve. Even as Rogers tried to become closer to his staff via organisational discussion, a fifth of his team urged him to get even closer. True listening is taking the good with the bad, absorbing criticism even when it is direct and personal—and even when the people who offer it are your coworkers.

A initiative intended at bringing the company's corporate principles life for its employees at Exelon, an energy supplier based in Chicago, resulted in a very intimate kind of organisational discussion. Values statements are sometimes rejected as mere rhetoric since they fail to establish intimacy. As a result, Exelon experimented with how it communicated about diversity, which is a key value: It utilised a series of short video clips of senior executives speaking unscripted and very directly about what diversity meant to them—no bother, no pretence, no high production qualities. They discussed race, sexual orientation, and other topics that are rarely discussed in the workplace. Ian McLean, an Exelon financial officer at the time, talked about growing up in Manchester, England, as the son of a working-class family and felt the sting of discrimination. In response to a question about a time when he felt "different," he described working in a bank with mostly upper-class colleagues: "My accent was different... I wasn't included, wasn't invited, and I was made to believe I wasn't quite as intelligent as they were... I never want anyone else to feel that [way] around me." Employees are impressed by such straightforward anecdotes.

Interactivity: Dialogue Promotion

A personal conversation, by definition, is a two- or more-person exchange of remarks and questions. Obviously, the sound of one person talking is not a discussion. The same may be said about organisational conversations, in which executives converse with rather than at employees. The dialogue becomes open and flowing rather than closed and directive as a result of the involvement. It means eschewing monologue's simplicity in favour of dialogue's unexpected energy. Interactivity reinforces and builds on intimacy: Efforts to narrow gaps between employees and their leaders will fail if people don't have the skills and institutional support they need to speak up and (where appropriate) respond.

A trend toward more interaction is partly due to a shift in communication routes. For decades, technology made supporting contact inside companies of any scale difficult or impossible. Print and broadcast, in example, were employed by corporations to gain size and efficiency in their communications, but they only worked in one direction. However, new channels have thrown that one-way system into disarray. Leaders and their workers may use social technologies to infuse a corporate environment with the style and spirit of personal communication.

However, achieving interactivity is more than simply a question of locating and implementing the appropriate technologies. The need to support social media with social thought is just as vital, if not more so. Too frequently, the dominant culture of a company works against any attempt to make business communication a two-way street. The temptation for many CEOs and managers to utilise every media available to them as if it were a megaphone has proven difficult to resist. Leaders at other firms, on the other hand, have cultivated a truly interactive culture—values, norms, and behaviours that establish a welcome environment for dialogue.

Consider Cisco Systems for an example of how interaction works. Cisco, as it happens, manufactures and distributes a variety of social technology-related devices. Internally, its employees have investigated the advantages of permitting high-quality back-and-forth communication. TelePresence, for example, replicates a face-to-face conference by transmitting video streams across locations. Multiple big displays provide a wraparound appearance, and specially constructed conference tables (in an ideal configuration) mirror one another, giving the impression that everyone is sitting at the same table. This is, in some ways, a more sophisticated form of a web-based video chat, with none of the delays or glitches that are common with online video. What's more, it masters the crucial issue of visual size. When Cisco engineers examined remote contacts, they discovered that if a person's on-screen picture is less than 80% of their real size, individuals who view the image are less engaged in conversing with that person. Participants in TelePresence appear to be life-size and may look each other in the eyes.

TelePresence is a complex technological instrument, yet it allows for the restoration of instantaneous and spontaneous give-and-take. Cisco's senior vice president of operations, processes, and systems, Randy Pond, believes that this sort of contact provides the advantage of the "full" discussion, which he demonstrated with an anecdote. One day, while sitting at his workstation for a video conference, he could see video feeds of many coworkers on his computer screen when he made a remark to the group, and one of the participants "just dropped his head in his hands"—probably in dismay, and likely not realising Pond could see him. Pond explained, "I said, 'I can see you.'" "'Tell me if you disagree.'" Pond was then able to contact his sceptical colleague in order to acquire the "whole storey." A less involved type of communication may have ultimately provided similar knowledge, but it would have done it in a considerably less efficient manner.

Cisco's CEO, John Chambers, is at the centre of the company's communication culture, holding different forums to remain in touch with employees. He hosts a "birthday conversation" every other month, for example, available to any Cisco employee whose birthday falls within the appropriate two-month period. Senior executives aren't invited since their presence could prevent others from speaking freely. Chambers also films a video blog approximately once a month, which is a quick, improvised message sent to all workers through e-mail. He can communicate to his employees immediately, informally, and without a script when he uses video; it conveys immediacy and develops trust. Despite the fact that a video blog is essentially one-way, Chambers and his colleagues have made it participatory by asking workers to provide video messages as well as written comments.

Expanding Employee Roles Through Inclusion

Personal communication is, at its finest, an equal-opportunity endeavour. It allows participants to share ownership of the discussion's content. As a result, individuals are able to bring their own ideas—and, indeed, their hearts and souls—to the debate. Organizational dialogue, on the other hand, encourages workers to contribute to the creation of content that tells a company's narrative. Inclusive leaders convert workers into full-fledged discussion partners by include them among a company's official or quasi-official communicators. As a result, such leaders increase the amount of emotional involvement that employees bring to the workplace as a whole.

To the characteristics of closeness and engagement, inclusion adds a crucial dimension. In contrast to intimacy, which focuses on leaders' attempts to become closer to their workers, inclusion emphasises on the role that employees play in that process. It also broadens the concept of interaction by allowing employees to contribute their own ideas, rather than merely parrying those of others, through official business channels. It empowers them to act as content suppliers on the front lines.

Top executives and professional communicators control content production under the traditional corporate communication paradigm, and retain a tight grip on what employees write or say on official business channels. When a culture of inclusion emerges, however, engaged employees may take on additional responsibilities such as generating content and serving as brand ambassadors, thought leaders, and storytellers.

Ambassadors for the brand

Employees that are enthusiastic about their company's products and services become live brand ambassadors. This may and will happen naturally—many individuals are passionate about what they do for a career and will promote it on their own time. However, some businesses deliberately encourage this type of conduct. Coca-Cola, for example, has established an official ambassadorship programme to encourage workers to promote the Coke brand and product range in their words and actions. Employees may use the Coke intranet to access services like a platform that connects them to company-sponsored volunteer opportunities. The program's core is a list of nine ambassadorial actions, which include helping the firm "win at the point of sale" (for example, by cleaning up store displays in retail outlets), relaying sales leads, and reporting instances where a merchant has ran out of a Coke product.

Leaders of thought

Companies may hire consultants or in-house specialists to produce speeches, articles, white papers, and other materials in order to gain market leadership in a knowledge-based industry. However, the most inventive thinking is typically found deep within a company, where employees create and test new products and services. Empowering such individuals to produce and distribute thought-leadership content may be a rapid and effective approach to improve a company's reputation among important industry players. Juniper Networks has supported programmes in recent years to attract prospective thought leaders out of their laboratories and offices and into public settings where industry professionals and customers can see them strut their stuff. Engineers at the firm are working on the next generation of systems silicon and hardware and can provide valuable insight into emerging trends. Juniper sends them to national and international technology conferences and arranges for them to meet with clients at company-run briefing centres to express their viewpoint to relevant audiences.

Storytellers

People are used to hearing corporate communication experts deliver business stories, but nothing beats hearing a narrative straight from the trenches. The message comes to life when employees talk candidly about their personal experiences. EMC, the computer storage behemoth, constantly seeks out anecdotes from its employees. Leaders turn to them for suggestions on how to enhance corporate performance as well as opinions about the firm. The goal is to foster the belief that thoughts from all walks of life are accepted. For instance, in 2009, the firm released The Working Mother Experience, a 250-page coffee-table book created by and for EMC employees about how to be a successful EMC employee while also being a mom. Frank Hauck, then the executive vice president of worldwide marketing and customer quality, championed the initiative, which was started on the front lines. It's not uncommon for a large corporation like EMC to develop a vanity project like this, but this was not a corporate marketing effort; instead, it was a peer-driven initiative lead by workers. Several hundred EMC employees also maintain blogs, many of which are accessible to the public, in which they share their uncensored opinions about work and technology.

Of course, inclusion implies that CEOs relinquish some control over how the firm is portrayed to the outside world. However, cultural and technological developments have already weakened such power. Whether you like it or not, anybody in your company's reputation may be tarnished (or polished) straight from her cubicle by e-mailing an internal document to a reporter, a blogger, or even a group of friends—or by publishing her opinions in an online forum. As a result, inclusive leaders are turning a necessity into a virtue. Volcano Corporation's CEO, Scott Huennekens, claims that a more relaxed attitude to communication has made organisational life less suffocating and more effective than before. The unfettered flow of knowledge fosters a more liberated mindset. Some businesses make an effort to establish some fundamental standards. Employees at Infosys, for example, are told that they can disagree but not to be unpleasant, despite the fact that the company admits it has no control over their involvement in social media.

And, as many executives have learned, a system of employee self-regulation typically fills the gap left by top-down management. Someone makes an outlandish comment, the community reacts, and the overall mood returns to the middle.

Pursuing an Agenda with Intentionality

If it's genuinely rich and fulfilling, a personal discussion will be open but not aimless; the participants will have some idea of what they want to accomplish. They might be trying to entertain, convince, or learn from one other. A discourse will either meander or run into a blind alley if there is no such aim. Even the loosest and most digressive kinds of conversation are given structure and meaning by intent. This idea also applies to conversations within organisations. The numerous voices that contribute to a company's communication process must eventually converge on a unified view of what communication is for. To put it another way, the discourse that takes place within a company should be guided by a common agenda that is in line with the organization's strategic goals.

In one important way, intentionality varies from the other three aspects of organisational dialogue. While intimacy, interaction, and inclusion all help to open up the flow of information and ideas inside a firm, intentionality gives the process a sense of closure: It helps leaders and workers to take strategic action as a result of the push and pull of debate and discussion.

Leaders must communicate strategic concepts not merely by proclaiming them, but also by explaining them—by creating consent rather than forcing acquiescence. Leaders in this new paradigm communicate with employees widely and openly on the vision and logic that underpin executive decision-making. As a consequence, employees at all levels get a comprehensive understanding of their company's position in its competitive environment. In other words, they become knowledgeable about organisational strategy.

Allowing workers to participate in the development of the company's governing strategy is one approach to help them comprehend it. Infosys' executive team has begun include a diverse group of employees in the company's yearly strategy-development process. When Infosys management started developing an organisational plan for the 2011 fiscal year in late 2009, they asked individuals from every rank and division to participate. They specifically invited workers to submit suggestions on "the key transformative themes that we see affecting our consumers," said to Kris Gopalakrishnan, a cofounder and executive cochairman. Infosys strategic strategists compiled a list of 17 trends based on those concepts, ranging from the expansion of new markets to a growing emphasis on environmental sustainability. They then set up a series of online forums where workers could discuss ways to link each trend to potential consumer solutions that the firm may provide. Bottom-up engagement was facilitated across the firm thanks to technology and social media.

In 2008, Kingfisher plc, the third-largest home improvement retailer in the world, embarked on a new strategy to turn a collection of traditionally separate business groups into "one team," aided in part by purposeful organisational dialogue. To kick off the initiative, corporate leaders hosted a three-day event for retail executives in Barcelona. On the second day, everyone took part in a 90-minute Share at the Marketplace session, which was designed to resemble a traditional Mediterranean or Middle Eastern market. One set of participants, known as "suppliers," wore aprons and stood at one of 22 stalls, ready to make a presentation about a business technique established by individuals in their respective parts of the Kingfisher organisation. They were essentially merchants of ideas.

Another group, comprised of members of the executive committee, acted as facilitators, ambling around the aisles and offering words of advice and encouragement. The third and largest group acted as buyers, travelling from stall to stall, inspecting the "merchandise," and occasionally "buying" one of the concepts. Buyers might write up to five checks to pay for suppliers' goods using special chequebooks supplied for the purpose. Such transactions were meaningless outside of the session, but they sent a powerful message to the suppliers: What you're saying is amazing. The marketplace's core concept was peer-to-peer exchange of best practises in a casual, dirty, and noisy setting. However, the goal was to utilise dialogue as a means to an end—to use it to establish strategic alignment among a heterogeneous collection of people.

Every firm has a conversation going on, whether you realise it or not. That has always been the case, but today's debate has the ability to extend far beyond your walls, and you have little control over it. Smart leaders figure out how to utilise dialogue to control the flow of information in an open and honest way. One-way broadcast messaging is a thing of the past, and attractive marketing materials have about as much of an impact on employees as they do on consumers. People, on the other hand, will pay attention to communication that is personal, engaging, inclusive, and purposeful.

9 781802 768824